H●US$E
F🔥RE

**How to Be a Red-Hot Real Estate Millionaire
with a Wealth of Time and Money to Burn**

HOU$E
FIRE

SO YOU CAN ACHIEVE
Financial Independence
and Retire Early

ALAN COREY

author of *A Million Bucks by 30*

House Money Publishing

ISBN
    Print: 978-1-7366183-0-1
    eBook: 978-1-7366183-1-8
    Audiobook: 978-1-7366183-2-5

Published by House Money Publishing, LLC

Contact the author at www.TheHouseOfAC.com and Alan@TheHouseOfAC.com.

Contents

Introduction

Let's FIRE Up This Blaze

Here is your new goal: Don't dream about being rich, get rich dreaming. And you know what's rich? You—when you achieve financial independence and retire early. It's called FIRE, get it? Financial Independence and Retire Early?

Good news, I'm here to help you build your FIRE, which I will simply reference as FIRE moving forward. This book will get you to make money in your sleep, which then gives you the freedom to chase your dreams. I promise you that.

It's that simple, and I'm not a crazy real estate guru trying to sell you a life of luxury. You are on your own for creating whatever life you desire. I'll give you the recipe, sure, but you still have to mix the ingredients together and light it on FIRE like Bananas Foster.

Think of me as your Gordon Ramsay guiding you through a Thanksgiving meal, and I'll treat you as a *Kitchen Nightmares* amateur chef looking to be verbally berated, if that works for you. You'll come out on the other end probably hating me throughout the process, but you'll have a sweet five-course meal—or more accurately a modest Michelin-rated rental portfolio, and one that kicks off some tasty cash flow that you can live off.

A little about you first.

- Do you hate your job?

- Or is your dream job one that barely pays a livable wage, so, instead, you work somewhere less fulfilling and more soul-crushing in order to make ends meet?

- Is your real dream to work for yourself, but you want a financial cushion before you really go after it?

- Do you see no way you can ever stop working because the bills never end and the salary never is high enough and, thus, your true calling is forever put on the back burner for another day?

Or do you fantasize often about a complicated evil revenge plot on your wicked boss, who actually asks you to do responsible tasks, but you feel is a prick because this boss is in charge of you five days a week, and sometimes on the weekend? And to get back at this creep, you daydream your retribution by quitting at the worst time ever in order to create maximum havoc so the boss has a stress-induced panic attack, which reveals their true incompetence to the CEO?

And then this implausible series of sadistic events makes the CEO have an epiphany that the whole company was actually relying on your incredibly well-rounded skill set this entire time and that if the CEO had to do everything over again that they should have given you all the recognition and promotions over the last five years rather than that sad sack in a monkey suit riding in back of an ambulance?

Sound familiar? Well, you are reading the right book at the right time (and also possibly should invest in a therapist).

Okay, fine, I was projecting. It was me that had those thoughts, and, yes, I did invest in a therapist. As you'll figure out shortly, I found a highly achievable way to leave my forty-hour-a-week job on a good note along with a creative way to pay my therapist bills. But if you connected with me at all during my rant, well, we must be kindred spirits, and I already like you.

If you read that and think I'm an insane lunatic with authority figure issues, well, you must be my therapist. But what matters is that I got it all worked out, and I'm going to share the formula with you for both your financial wealth and mental health.

- If you worry about your retirement or are concerned if you have enough saved up, I'll walk you down the path on how to answer that.

- If you are frozen with fear because you have a hunk of savings doing nothing but sitting in a checking account because you are not sure what to do with it, well, I'll thaw out that inaction and set you up with a plan.

- If you don't know what debt you should pay off first, then you'll be excited that my answer might be you don't pay off the debt. Now what other financial book gives that advice? I knew I would eventually win you over.

As a wise man, or most likely a wise woman, once said, a journey of a thousand miles starts with a single step, and this book is your first step on a journey not of a thousand miles but on an entirely new way of looking at your financial future. The best part is that by the end of this book, you're going to be able to go out and literally set your life on FIRE!

I'm going to show you exactly how to acquire rental properties and start you on the path to a truly life-altering and manageable real estate investing career and, thus, create a jealous-worthy life of financial independence and retiring early. Not only that, but I'm going to convince you that you absolutely can do it.

How do I know? Because I've done it myself, and I've helped many others just like you do it too. I can successfully live off the rental income of a handful of properties for the rest of my life—if I want to. I'm free to work on projects I want to work on, and I'm free to turn down work just because I'm not in the mood to deal with the effort it may take, all thanks to a system I call House FIRE.

That's my big promise to you. By reading this book, you're going to have the ability to go out and find your first property to invest in. This first step as an investor will give you the tools to do whatever you want to do: to give you some much-needed diversification in your investment portfolio, or to retire earlier than you ever thought possible, or to grow a real estate empire of hundreds of properties, or to provide you some extra income to support an obscure expensive hobby like gold-leafing bald eagle eggs.

It doesn't matter what your dreams are, because whatever they are, the real estate path to FIRE that I lay out for you gives you those options. However, I wish it were only as simple as me making a big promise. In order for this promise to come to life, I'd like you to make me a promise in return. Sound fair?

Don't worry, it's a simple promise. I want you to promise to follow the instructions in this book—my recipe on how to cook the effing turkey (read that again with a Gordon Ramsay accent). I need you to actually set a goal for yourself and take action.

I'll explain in short order how to make these dreams a reality, but we have got to be a team. Reading this book and then just putting it away on your beautiful floating bookshelf is not going to change your financial outlook in any positive way (but no doubt this jazzy book cover will really pull the whole room together).

If you do the steps I've laid out in this book and just follow the freakin' recipe, then you're going to pleasantly surprise Future You. You know, Future You, the person who has so much passive income that you can get rid of your 9-to-5 day job. Future You, who thanks Past You for reading this book and actually doing something about it. If Present You wants to truly impress Future You, the best way is to gift Future You a strong financial portfolio of rental properties.

Now getting that first piece of real estate property might seem like a giant hurdle to get over, yet when you do, you'll find that by your third property it is so easy you could almost do it in your sleep. And guess what, it's just the introduction of the book and you already learned that landlords make money in their slumber. But stay awake for now, because Future You wants to tell Present You to keep crackin' on as there are some good ideas packed in here to help you achieve this get-rich-while-dreaming thing.

What You Can Expect from This Book

Before we talk details, let me lay out exactly what this book is—or maybe I should start with what this book *isn't*.

Fair warning, this book is not a nuts-and-bolts explanation about looking through the newspaper or online forums and finding motivated home seller ads to get an amazing off-market property. This book is not going to be a course on phone etiquette or sales to nickel-and-dime struggling homeowners to secure a bargain buy-and-hold rental property.

I'm not going to dive into excruciating detail on property analysis, conservative savings withdrawal rate calculations for early retirement, ideal legal entities to skirt tax and inheritance law, or try to digest any complicated tax code. I know, phew, right? And I'm not going to pump you full of motivational quotes.

We may touch on these subjects and I may have a few relevant quotes from people you've never heard of, sure. But this book is the big picture. I'm going to show you how to look at real estate investing, how to *think* about real estate investing to get you to financial independence. I'll teach you how to actually create a road map that's going to lead you to those first few deals and why those early deals matter.

Through my personal journey as well as examples from others, I'm going to walk you from the basic starting point of House FIRE to becoming a savvy and, most importantly, a property-owning investor able to say adios to any corporate gig. If I'm a success, you will catch FIRE and thank me for it.

Think of this book as your plan to build a retirement foundation. I'll get into this more later, but keep in mind that you can't build a massive skyscraper without a foundation. This book and the properties it's going to empower you to buy will act as a solid foundation for your future financial well-being and to support as large or small a real estate investing career as you desire. You can even autopilot the whole thing with a property manager if you want to let real estate work for you completely hands-off.

Okay, I know you are probably asking, what exactly is FIRE? FIRE stands for Financial Independence, Retire Early. It's to be free of paycheck shackles. Of course, you can continue earning a paycheck if you like, but you don't have to. You aren't beholden to having a day job to pay for your housing, meals, transportation, entertainment, and more.

The growing FIRE movement is about building a war chest of savings or reliable passive income called F-U money, which, when once achieved, you get the pleasure of saying those words to your boss and then you can live a sweet sweet life of early retirement or brazen bridge burning (if you so desire).

You want to start down the path of not having to work a 9-to-5, right? Good, you are now thinking like the great human think tank and the terrible-haircut-wearing front man of the mid-'90s emo band The Prodigy when he sang about being a firestarter. But I'm guessing his motivations were more around arson and literal bridge burning than savvy financial planning, but that's the beauty of FIRE—you get to pursue whatever you may desire once you achieve it.

Now, remember, this is your financial future we are embarking on, and it can be a bumpy road. But that's okay. I'll be your copilot to help make it as smooth a ride as possible and navigate the twists and turns. But the final question you have to ask yourself is this: Do you want to be the bus driver or the passenger on your journey to FIRE? I'm about to give you the keys to the bus, so I hope you brought your beaded seat cover and Christmas tree air-freshener or it's going to be an uncomfortable ride.

Who Am I?

Before we dive in, let me give you a quick intro to myself just so you know who this Alan Corey guy is and why I have the audacity to try and instruct you.

I'm an entrepreneur, motivational speaker, and author of *The Subversive Job Search: How to Overcome a Lousy Job, Sluggish Economy, and Useless Degree to Create a Six-Figure Career.* My successful book tells readers how to create a six-figure career from nothing. If you want to get a raise at work or want to switch careers, that's a book for you.

I accumulated a million-dollar net worth by the age of twenty-eight while living in New York City and shared my personal finance success story in my first book, *A Million*

Bucks by 30. If you want to learn about the basics of financial planning and creative ways of living below your means, that's for you.

So I've published two books on making money, and this is my third on that same subject. I quite obviously like teaching people how to make some cash. Before you say it, I've yet to make much money writing books, though, so I probably won't write a book on that.

I've also conducted finance seminars to twenty- and thirtysomethings in New York City and at colleges around the country. I've been fortunate to have been featured in *Fast Company* magazine as a Fast 50 Rising Star and in *Money* magazine as a Millionaire in the Making, and was profiled in *US News & World Report* for my unconventional money-saving techniques.

The *New York Times* Real Estate section put my flip on their front page when I completed a $1.1 million sale of one of my buildings to real estate mogul and *Shark Tank* regular Barbara Corcoran. Additional profiles have appeared in the *New York Post, Time Out New York, Georgia Magazine,* and on NPR's *The Bryant Park Project* and *Talk of the Nation.* I was the page A1 above-the-fold lead story in the *Atlanta Journal-Constitution* about being a real estate whiz kid back when people still read newspapers.

But I'm older now. So with my time living the adult life, I've helped get a Manhattan-based real estate start-up acquired by Airbnb; I cofounded a real estate sign installation start-up in Atlanta; and I own a property management company, head a real estate brokerage team, am a principal in a private equity real estate firm that manages over $30 million in real estate. I personally own over sixty rental units and am partners on another 100 doors. Also, I literally wrote the book on House FIRE, so I consider myself an expert on the subject. I've got a bit of a real estate addiction, you can see.

Am I going to teach you how to start multiple businesses to satisfy your ADD or teach you how to feed your narcissism by accumulating press stories? No, but the financial independence part of FIRE allows me to pursue all these crazy ideas I have for myself and do things that I could not have done if I didn't have an alternative source of income to support me.

And guess what? Occasionally those pipe dreams I pursue pan out and make me more money so I can do other new ideas and chase bigger dreams. Yes, I'm still talking about getting rich dreaming. If I was chained to a desk working a 9-to-5, there is no way I would have been able to accomplish these feats.

Listen, at the end of the day I'm going to teach you how to acquire something more important than money and that is how to acquire more time in your day to do the things that please you. So if this is not enough proof that reaching FIRE through real estate is a noble pursuit, well, then, you are the numskull who bought a book about subjects that have no relation to the goals you are trying to accomplish. And you make my inner Gordon Ramsay have not so nice things to say to you.

Listen, I'm not a genius who has discovered some secret key. I've done what others before me have done, and I've been very lucky in my pursuit as well. Chances are you'll have some luck, too, owning a few properties because cool things will start to happen. But because I did something, and actively followed through on a few investments, I built a foundation to support my desires. Now it's your turn.

1

"Hey, Alan, go over that FIRE thing again. I didn't read the introduction, and I have a burning desire to know what you're talking about."

"Uhh uhh, cool. FIRE! FIRE! FIRE!" is definitely my favorite Beavis and Butt-Head saying, and I would like to think they were talking my kind of FIRE. Once again FIRE stands for financial independence and retire early, and those cartoon dudes were probably thinking about their future retirement when they chanted that from their piss-stained couch.

I know the FIRE acronym doesn't really roll off the tongue, but I didn't make it up so don't blame me. I'm way more creative than that.

The basic FIRE doctrine is that you try to have enough savings that you can live off those savings forever. The majority of the advice in the FIRE movement is about how to increase those savings by being super frugal and living well below your means, and then dumping everything you can into a low-cost diversified mutual fund. Now this is a great strategy if you like going to cocktail parties and having no one interested in talking to you. People can only take so much couponing and conservative mutual-fund investment conversation.

I know this because for ten years I used to be that obsessive cheapskate who lived off free happy-hour peanuts and refillable soft drinks, but I couldn't live that life forever. I know there are some introverts saying, "Slow down, Skippy, that sounds like heaven," and to those people I recommend they read my first book, *A Million Bucks by 30*. It's about how I lived in Manhattan on just 31% of my $40,000 income and pinched every possible penny to eventually live the FIRE life at age twenty-eight.

There are benefits to this approach, and it definitely can lead you to FIRE, but, at the same time, it can drastically chip away at your soul. Everyone wants to go on vacations, wants to eat at the hot new restaurant, and wants to splurge every now and then on something frivolous. Well, I'm writing this book to do that because the way I teach FIRE is without all the obsessive-compulsive scrimping and saving. Plus, being a wallflower at parties is not in my nature.

Yes, it's true. I've figured out a way to FIRE and live in abundance rather than squeezing every penny out of every bulk ramen noodle purchase. That sounds like a little better way to retire, eh? I've figured out a way where you actually make more money in early retirement than you did at your peak earning years at your day job. That sounds pretty interesting, right?

I've figured out a way to basically rock early retirement so hard you can knock down a rain forest to build your own pickle-ball court and charge other retiree suckas $50 an hour to play on it. That sounds like being a dick, huh? Well, maybe, but regardless if that is the life you envision for yourself as an early retiree, I will get you there.

So what is this special way of doing FIRE? What is that secret ingredient to living large in retirement with an optional dash of dickishness? What is the unique code to crack to get to this utopia? Well, I really hope you didn't read the title of this book because, otherwise, I've lost the surprise factor. But assuming you haven't, well here it is—

and it's called (drum roll, guitar solo, harp jam)—

—wait for it, audio snippet of Hugh Laurie, dang, I apologize, the bassist wants to do his thing, now comes the David Byrne feature solo.

It sounds like there are sirens going off outside and that's not part of the song, it's just the studio is in a basement of a fire station. Well anyway, it's called *House FIRE!*

Yes, my way of living large in retirement is to House FIRE, or having enough passive income, or cash flow from real estate, that I no longer worry about stock market swings or where the closest kids-eat-free buffets are. I can live like a Lord of the Manor or, more accurately, like a multiple-property-owning landlord.

At the end of this book you will have a firm grasp on why houses, rental houses to be specific, are going to be your fastest and most lucrative path to FIRE. When I'm done mentoring you, you will be free to wallpaper your rentals with F-U money. And although House FIRE runs counter to typical how-to-retire-early financial advice, you will come around and see that it does indeed make the most sense to do it my way. You may have been brainwashed by well-meaning financial gurus to reduce expenses as much as possible, but I'm not opposed to being unconventional to get unconventional results, are you?

To start, House FIRE replaces the "having enough savings to last me until I die" idea with the "having enough passive income I could live forever and never run out of money" plan. The latter makes for better cocktail conversation. Am I right? If someone has that knowledge, I'd want to corner that guy and pick his brain all night until he tells me to buy his book and leave him alone. For now, buy me a drink and I'll keep yapping.

So conventional early retirement wisdom says in order to FIRE you first figure out your FIRE number. And everything moving forward works around that number. It's simple math to figure out your FIRE number, or the total amount you need in your savings to be able to drop the f-bomb around your place of employment with no fear of repercussions.

You figure out what your total annual living expenses are by adding up your annual rent or mortgage payment, food costs, transportation expenses, entertainment and vacation budget, healthcare fees, and anything else that is a must-have expense in your life. You really gotta dig through your checking account transactions and credit card statements and get a good idea what you or you and your family spend in an average year. This is important to calculate as it really puts a spotlight on your questionable porn and corn purchases (really the only question is why are they always bought together?).

Anyway, maybe you have $50,000 a year in nonquestionable expenses. Maybe it's $75,000 a year. Or maybe it's $25,000 if you sell two cars, bike everywhere, and knit your own clothes from discarded barbershop hair trimmings. You just have to envision the lifestyle you want for the rest of your life and figure out what it will cost per annum.

Great, you got your budget for your annual expenses? Now just multiply that number by 25. That's your FIRE number. Here's an example:

	Typical Personal Expenses	
	Monthly	Annual
Utilities		
Phone	100	1,200
Internet	150	1,800
Electric	75	900
Water	50	600
Gas	45	540
Transportation		
Car 1 Payment	350	4,200
Car 2 Payment	150	1,800
Gas	100	1,200
Parking	40	480
Repairs	75	900
Housing		
Rent/Mortgage	1,000	12,000
Loans		
Student Loans	1,000	12,000
Entertainment		
Streaming	40	480
In Person	150	1,800
Gifts	25	300
Food		
Grocery	350	4,200
Delivery	100	1,200
Restaurants	200	2,400
Total	**4,000**	**48,000**
		x 25
FIRE Number		**$1,200,000**

Now, it doesn't take an Alan Corey to figure out the lower you make your expenses, the lower your FIRE number is going to be. But it does take Alan Corey to tell you that if you are cutting expenses, then you are probably reducing your lifestyle along with it. That's not how I want to wheelchair roll into my grave. I want to ride a diamond-encrusted hover board off a private jet somewhere over a secluded beach and be ceremoniously tossed from 10,000 feet through levitating fire hoops into my grave. That's retirement living and House FIRE dying, mi amigo. I want my expenses to go UP in retirement not go down. And, well, you can do that with House FIRE.

But first, let's go back to traditional FIRE advice so you can fully comprehend the genius behind House FIRE. Three main variations of FIRE are built around this FIRE number: FIRE, Lean FIRE, and Fat FIRE. Those variations are built around what your living expense budget is and corresponding FIRE number.

If you prefer to have one foot into retirement and the other foot in the working world, then maybe Barista FIRE and Coast FIRE is something for you, which I'll cover in a bit.

Typical FIRE breathers, though, once they hit their FIRE number in savings, quit their job and withdraw 4% a year from their savings. In the previous example, you live off $48,000 a year, then you have to save a ridiculous $1,200,000. This is where the FIRE movement turns off most people. You have to live below your means and also be a millionaire? What's the fun in that?

And this is where most of the world freezes on the concept of FIRE and says "not for me." FIRE evangelicals try to convince people FIRE is great because you have to live below your means and save over a million dollars. What's the point of being a millionaire, then, if you can't live like one?

Don't worry, though, a famous paper from Trinity University creatively called "The Trinity Study" found if you FIRE'd at the worst possible time in history and then had to live off your savings after your horrendous market timing, you would still be able to live off 4% of your savings, or $48,000 a year. So you are planning for your worst case scenario with the 4% rule and if you want to be ultra-conservative then you'll be safe at a 4% withdrawal rate. However a 5.5% rate will usually suffice and give you a nice buffer to cover emergencies if you think you'll have average timing and expect to get average returns. That extra 1.5% would give you a more manageable $66,000 to spend annually. You pick your risk tolerance for the withdrawal rate, but it's a sliding scale between 4% and 5.5%.

So the example I presented is your typical FIRE lifestyle, with roughly $48,000 to $50,000 in annual expenses. Considering the average salary in the United States is $56,516, this is pretty good living in retirement. If you want to FIRE in this range but currently live in a high cost of living city, moving to a lower cost of living city may be in the cards. Or you wait until your kids are off to college and are no longer eating you out of house and home.

But what if you don't have a ton of savings or don't want to move and don't have kids and are just starting to learn about FIRE later in life?

The typical guidance is then to focus on Lean FIRE, which sits at the far left end of the FIRE spectrum. If you can live off just $25,000 a year, then you only need to save $625,000 ($25,000 x 25) in liquid savings.

Now, understand that it's tough to live off $25,000 unless you want to be a hippie who hits bongs and bongos all day. I kid, I kid. I used to have white-guy dreadlocks and live in Eugene, Oregon, so I know this life well. But living off expenses this low, you will most likely have to sell your car and ride a bike everywhere, potentially replace your house with a yurt, and maybe grow your own vegetables off unused federal property along the side of the highway. Nothing wrong with extreme frugal living, and I admire the restraint it takes and the benefits it brings to Mother Nature—she needs it.

"But, Alan," you ask, "what if I have a modicum of sense and don't want to have white-guy dreadlocks or garden next to prisoners picking up trash? And, Alan, I know there is no way I can save $625,000 with my student loan debts and car payments."

No worries. There are other variations of FIRE for different retirement lifestyles and situations.

Barista FIRE might be a good fit for you if you want to level up a bit from Lean FIRE. This flavor of Guy Fieri, I mean FIRE, means you have enough funds to leave your full-time job and get by with a part-time job. Maybe you work just enough hours at a coffee chain to get your health insurance provided or you work a few hours a week as a consultant or teacher to make ends meet. Maybe you have a spouse who works while you early retire. Or you can be a bit nomadic and travel to take on high-demand seasonal employment opportunities around the world. That's a great way to retire early for sure, but it still requires you to grunt work against your will a few times of the year most likely. It's better than grunt working forty hours a week, I suppose. I mention it so you know that it is an option.

The more financially well-off seem to favor Coast FIRE and Fat FIRE. Coast FIRE is where you have hit your FIRE number but keep working. You can just spend what you make each year, work if you want, and coast into retirement without worrying about adding to your savings anymore. Coast FIRE is for those achievers who probably benefited from a high-income job for most of their career or got a generous windfall in stock options, inheritance, or are just naturally financially prudent and have lived a pretty low-expense life throughout their entire career.

Finally, the living large in retirement end and the far right side of the spectrum is Fat FIRE, which identifies itself with $100,000 in annual expenses a year or more and Morbidly Obese FIRE, or MO FIRE, with a $200,000 in annual expenses target. I am honestly not making these names up, but I do approve of them. And it is at these levels and above where House FIRE lives.

But you know what FIRE term I did make up? HELLFIRE, or Having Every Luxury in Life in Financial Independence and Retiring Early. It's the new highest-end version of FIRE that can most easily be achieved via House FIRE.

I define HELLFIRE as having $500,000 in living expenses covered a year, or to limit spending to $41,666 a month. (I'm well-aware 666 and HELL might not be the best branding, but sometimes you just got to dance with the devil to reach your dreams, my friend.)

Name	Annual Expenses	FIRE Number
Lean FIRE	$ 25,000	$ 625,000
FIRE	$ 50,000	$ 1,250,000
Fat FIRE	$100,000	$ 2,500,000
MO FIRE	$200,000	$ 5,000,000
HELLFIRE	$500,000	$12,500,000

Now, I know not everyone wants or needs this opulent lifestyle to be financially independent. I haven't unlocked the HELLFIRE achievement yet, but I'm on pace to get there by age fifty-five, which is seven years before the average retirement age of sixty-two.

Without the House FIRE approach, I'd probably get there at about age 198 best case scenario, not my prime pickle-ball years for sure. But feel free to buy multiple copies of this book to help me get there a little quicker because according to the devil's "Trident Study," doing this will bring you good luck or it brings a fiddler down to Georgia. It's one or the other, I don't remember.

But here is what I do know: The fact that these varieties of FIRE exist means that tons of people are channeling Johnny Paycheck and taking their jobs and shoving them. And it's one thing to sing it, but it's another to live it. And it's a truly awful thing to hear me sing it, which is why I just write about it. But to all these people who used the traditional ways to FIRE, I'm going to blow their minds about this better way to tell your job to shove it.

Did I mention yet that House FIRE is the crème de la crème of FIRE? I know you want me to get on with the details already. Just let me ramble a bit more. We covered the basics of typical FIRE planning. With that scene being set, you can effectively do a comparison between House FIRE and these other FIRE methods.

Trust me, I'm not just the cool uncle with financial conspiracy theories; this is real-life stuff. I'm now going to tell you why House FIRE says your FIRE number is a worthless metric. I'm going to teach you that House FIRE says don't pay off your student loan or car note early if you want to live larger later in life. I'm going to coach you why House FIRE also says plugging away and growing your mutual funds is not the best use of your money. And I'll impart the wisdom of House FIRE that says reducing your expenses is not necessary.

And finally, House FIRE makes it so you don't have to be a millionaire to retire early or be a financial independent. I just saw you breathe a sigh of relief, that's good. Now I know you are with me on this.

So let's see how House FIRE approaches the previous expense sheet we mapped out. Let's just look at the utility expenses.

Typical Personal Expenses		
	Monthly	Annual
Utilities		
Phone	100	1,200
Internet	150	1,800
Electric	75	900
Water	50	600
Gas	45	540
Total	420	5,040
		x 25
FIRE Number		**$126,000**

Someone who has $420 a month in utilities spends $5,040 a year covering these bills alone. To calculate one's FIRE number, or early retirement number, they need to save 25 times that amount, or $126,000. The portion of savings is then earmarked for lifetime supply of utilities for the early retiree.

But let's go deeper in these expenses and just focus on the $150 internet bill. In this example, internet is responsible for $1,800 a year in budget expenses. That means before you retire, you need to save 25 times this $1,800 annual expense, or $45,000. This is the conventional FIRE way of calculating if you can be financially free. You do this to all your monthly expenses.

If it was an option, the FIRE community would advise you to go to Costco and buy a lifetime supply of internet access for a discounted $35,000 before you give your ol' job the heave ho. You save $10,000 by doing that. But Costco can't do that for you. Costco isn't so great for bulk purchase of utilities it seems.

Well, FIRE advisors will tell you if you can't go to Costco to buy it and you can't save $45,000 for lifetime internet either, well, just adjust your lifestyle and live without internet. That's right, it's so easy you just run to the library every time you want to read unfunny memes emailed from your aunt. Also, who doesn't want to Netflix and chill with the Dewey Decimal System? This one life hack will save $45,000 in retirement just by streaming content during business hours at a public institution. Well, that's a pretty crappy retirement (and dating) life, IMHO.

But that's not what House FIRE tells you to do. House FIRE teaches that you can buy a lifetime supply of internet, and not only that, but because you bought a lifetime supply of internet, it will be an asset that increases in value over time. And if you like the way that sounds, it also doesn't cost you $45,000 or $35,000 or limit your email access around certain hours. House FIRE says you can achieve these advantages for only $25,000. How so?

Well, you save $25,000 first, duh. That's the secret first step. Then you use those savings to buy a house. That's the secret second step. Let's say this chunk of change is good enough for a 25% down payment on a $100,000 three-bedroom house in an okay neighborhood. It's also a house you can rent out for $1,000 a month.

After mortgage, insurance, taxes, and a budget for repairs, you end up paying $850 in expenses each month as a first-time landlord. And guess what? That leaves you a monthly cash flow of $150 a month. BOOM! Free internet for life. Cash flow $150 = internet bill $150. Who's the king bulk supplier now, Costco? I just ousted the FIRE movement's favorite store in two secret steps.

And being a real estate investor in the USA you get the ability to use tax depreciation to save on taxes for that rental income you are now earning. So what is tax depreciation? The tax gods at the IRS say a useful life of a real estate property is 27.5 years. So let's say you buy a house for $100,000. Maybe the land is worth $10,000 but the house itself is worth $90,000. Land doesn't depreciate, it will always be land and maintain its value of $10,000. But a house will wear down over time, which means you can write off the $90,000 value of the house over a span of 27.5 years. That leaves you with $3,272.72 a year in tax write-offs ($90,000/27.5), which breaks down to $272 a month.

That means on this rental property you don't pay taxes on the first $272 in profit you make each month. If you make $275 a month, then you only get taxed as if you are making $3 ($275 profit - $272 tax depreciation). But if you only make $150 a month cash flow, that means you pay no taxes at all. Pretty sweet deal, huh?

But what about the extra $122 in tax write-offs ($272 tax deduction - $150 cash flow = $122 unused tax write-off)? Well the good news is you can apply this extra tax deduction to any other real estate income you make, so it only comes into effect by owning multiple properties. Assuming you are in the 25% tax rate, reducing your tax burden elsewhere by $122 a month is about a $30 savings (122 a month x 25%). And that $30 in savings kills more than half of your $50 water bill.

And, of course, there are more advantages to owning real estate rentals. In this example, your tenant's rent also ends up paying down about $75 a month of principal on your mortgage balance each month. This $75 does not go directly in your pocket, but it is $75 of home equity added to your net worth each month, which reduces your fire number by $22,500 ($75 a month x 12 months x 25 years to get FIRE number).

You can continue to bill slay and FIRE number chop with just this one house, and it will continue to do so as long as you own the property.

Don't forget, rental income typically goes up about 3% each year. But your expenses probably go up about 2% to 2.5% each year. If you make an effort to reduce expenses by shopping around for different insurance rates or creating a more energy efficient home to reduce any landlord bills you are responsible for, it's not a stretch to say you can make about $10 more each year, or 1% increase in income on a $1,000 a month rental.

That means in two years that $50 water bill is hacked to its death since you already have $30 of it slayed with tax depreciation. In ten years, that rental increase will roundhouse kick your water bill to its demise, and your $40 streaming bill will be beautifully brought to its knees and executed. And by fast-forwarding time a bit, the principal paydown your tenant is paying goes up from about $75 to $100 a month and thus taking down another $25 bill with it. Talk about serial killing bills!

Now, when I eventually make the infomercial for *House FIRE*, this is the part I get to yell, "But, wait, there's more!"

This rental house will also be historically appreciating 3 to 4% a year, which means your $100,000 home is going to be worth $130,000 a decade later. So, to recap, you paid $25,000 to buy a house that appreciated by $30,000 in ten years. And plus you have your water, electric, grocery, and streaming bills covered. In another twenty years, the mortgage will be paid off by your tenant earning you about another $350 in bill killing ways.

There ain't no party like a House FIRE party because a House FIRE party don't stop. Am I right or am I right? Costco, you just a weak-ass pantry. (C'mon, you need to House FIRE just to be able to say that whenever you see their looming gray box of a building off the side of the highway.)

Now, besides flexing on Costco, what do you think happens if you buy more than one rental house? Or you find a place that gets more than a $150 cash flow? Or a property that appreciates more rapidly in value?

Or what will the results be if you start your House FIRE journey today instead of kicking the can down the road for two or three years? Well, refill my drink already, I have more to share before this lovely party host kicks us out and goes to bed.

Now let's quickly go back to the traditional advice one more time for comparison's sake. The boring old-school FIRE way is to pay off car loans and student loans and other debts first to get expenses down, and with money left over then you invest in stocks and mutual funds and other mind-numbing things. So what's wrong with that?

Let's do a quick illustration. A simple Google search tells me the following stats in good ol' America:

- Average car debt is $18,500,
- Average car payoff is five years,
- Average car loan rate is 5.27%,
- Average monthly car payment is $350,
- Average student loan debt is $30,000,
- Average student loan payoff is thirty years,
- Average student loan rate is 5.8%, and
- Average monthly student loan payment is $175.

Let's say if you work overtime at work that you can save $5,000 a year after covering all your current expenses plus the debts I just listed. That means in five years you could save $25,000. Which of the following three options would you want for your future self in just half a decade:

Option 1: No car debt because you aggressively paid it off in three years with your extra $5,000 in savings each year. That then allowed you to begin to aggressively pay off student loan debt starting in year three, and you got it down to $15,000 by the end of year 5. Your $25,000 that you spent now belongs to the car company and the student loan company. You now plan to erase the student loan debt paid off in about two more years and then you will start saving for a house.

Option 2: No student loan debt because you put all $5,000 extra each year to pay it off early. No car payment because you paid as scheduled, and it was going to take you five years to pay it off anyway. You spent $25,000 and it belongs to the car company and the student loan company. Now you spend the next three years to save up $25,000 to buy your first house.

Option 3: You make regular car payments and it is paid off since it's five years later and that was the term of the car note. With the $25,000 you saved up over time, you buy a $100,000 house at the end of year 5. That house has a $150 cash flow, which reduces the $175 student loan bill down to $25 a month for you. With a $25 rental increase to your tenant three years later, your cash flow now fully kills the entire $175 student loan charge. The $25,000 you spent still belongs to you because it was used as a down payment on a house you own.

So if you pick option 1, you still have debt and spent $25,000. If you pick option 2, you have no debt, but you spent $25,000 to get there. Option 3, you only have $900 of debt ($25 a month of payment for three years), but you kept your $25,000.

Umm, okay, so do you see now that House FIRE isn't get rich quick, but it's definitely faster than going with the other two options to work your way into financial independence? You see how options 1 and 2 are about reducing your expenses in order to reduce your FIRE number?

You see how in option 3 you have someone else paying off your student loan bills? And once that person eventually pays off your student loan in full, what happens? You have an unassigned $175 of cash flow and nowhere for it to go. Well, I guess you get to live larger in retirement with it. And then, eventually, the mortgage is paid off by the same tenant and you have even more moola to pamper your retirement pantaloons with. Jesus H. Real Estate, House FIRE life is a savior.

2

"Yes but, Alan, ya know, investing in hot market stocks and bonds through mutual funds sounds way easier than buying real estate."

It does take some effort to build a House FIRE, but it also takes tremendous effort to be a Walmart greeter until you die. I'm not trying to be disparaging; I'm trying to put it in perspective. A little up-front work now will pay huge dividends down the road. Or alternatively, you work until you die. Or work until you hit your FIRE number and hope you don't die before you reach it.

What is so magical about real estate anyway? Why are so many people into this particular form of investing? Why is the best plan of action to build a life around House FIRE so you can be financially independent and retire early?

Well, you can argue this one back and forth all day long. Certainly some people think the stock market is the only way to go or they feel that precious metals are the real deal or they love to invest in small business start-ups. Then, of course, the majority of people simply park their money in the bank or in a mutual fund managed by a 401(k) plan and do no other investing.

Well, as for the last one, it's my personal feeling that investing is a verb. That means that if I'm going to put my money into something, I want control over that something. There is absolutely nothing that gives you more control than real estate.

But, Alan, you might be thinking, the real estate market goes up and down and you can't control that.

That's certainly true, but that's also the case for every other type of investment. In your 401(k), for example, the only control you have is which of the twelve or so virtually identical funds you put your money in. If you buy and sell stocks, you're a passive investor only. You don't have any say over what happens with those companies, unless you happen to buy 51% or more of the actual company. Yes, at least with precious metals, you can lay your hands on gold, silver, platinum, and palladium bars, but it's still a simple buy-and-sell process.

Even as a venture capitalist, pumping money into somebody else's business, you will probably not have any say about the day-to-day operations unless you are investing real big money. So much money, you wouldn't be reading this book.

Yet think about a fourplex, or a rental property that has four individual units. You control how much you pay for it, you control how much you rent each unit for, you control who you rent to, you control what type of faucets you put in, and you control the sale. Every aspect of that investment is under your direct control, and, for me, that's a very attractive way to invest my money. Plus, you can get robbed and lose those precious gold bars, but no one is walking away with my fourplex because I lazily taped a security code to the side of the building.

Further, like precious metals, real estate has real-world intrinsic value. It's something people want and need. It occupies land, which is limited, and is something you can touch and feel. This is especially true for rental properties. People always need a place to live, and real estate is ideal for resisting economic change. But there is also no harm to doing multiple types of investing, and I actually encourage it.

FIRE is about protecting your nest egg too. You could sell some of your stocks to get started investing in real estate and then take the proceeds of your real estate investing once you FIRE to buy back some stocks. You might also want to flip a home or two to generate a large down payment so you can buy a more stable long-term rental to generate a larger amount of passive income.

It's completely smart to have a balanced portfolio and various real estate strategies so you don't have to pick one over the other. But the end goal, and best FIRE accelerant overall, is to have multiple leveraged long-term rental properties if you want to Fat FIRE or HELLFIRE.

What about finding tenants you may ask? Consider a booming real estate market where home prices are really high. Well, your average home buyer may not be able to get a mortgage, but they can rent the same house they want to buy with little problem. In a recession, when real estate prices might drop, it's harder to get a loan because the banks get very strict about credit scores and down payments, so people need to rent. And no matter what, there will always be folks who don't qualify for a home loan but who can pay the rent each month.

Current work-from-home trends allow employees to be nomadic and work from anywhere, and that temporary mindset allows freedom seekers to prefer renting over buying.

In the end, they just need a bed and shelter for a year or two, and then these laptop warriors are off doing it again in a new city. So be there to help them out with a decent place to stay and make some money at the same time.

Okay, I don't want to go on and on about the great news of rental properties. Since you're reading this book, you probably have already decided real estate is a tempting option for you. But I do want to take a closer look at the benefits of real estate.

The Long-term Financial Benefits

I want to illustrate how real estate is different from other asset classes. So I'm not going to focus on cash flow too much, which is an obvious result of buying rental property. Also, it's obvious that if you buy low and sell high, you're going to make a profit, which is true for most assets too.

No, what I want to focus on here is why I feel real estate is the best balance of all of your investing options to enable you to FIRE. A balance between risk and reward. See, real estate offers you two distinct advantages that most other investments don't. With real estate, there are tax benefits—several, in fact. With real estate, you get additional advantages if you use leverage to buy your properties.

In other words, the US tax code rewards you for being a real estate investor. You get to claim the cash flow as passive income—meaning, you only pay income tax and not FICA taxes. FICA is the Federal Insurance Contribution Act, where an employer typically takes 7.5% of your paycheck to fund Medicare and social security, which is not collected on rental income. Second, you get special tax depreciation write-offs on the rental building you own as previously mentioned. Third, there's even a tax loophole that lets you sell properties without paying a single penny of capital gains tax.

Yes, we're going to talk more about this later; I know you're just salivating to learn more. But let's focus on the exciting stuff for now: leveraging or borrowing money.

As for leverage, it's possible for you to walk into a bank, tell them you want to buy an investment, and get anywhere from 70 to as much as 75% of the purchase price in the form of a loan. Try walking into your bank next week and asking them to borrow $100,000 to buy stock in Amazon and see if they don't laugh you right out of the joint.

"Hold on there, cowboy! You say to me, isn't it better to pay cash? Isn't debt bad? Why would I want to borrow money to buy real estate to help with retirement? Also financial commentator and radio guy who hates debt, Dave Ramsey, told me so. He taught me mortgages are risky and I should stick to stocks and buying houses in cash."

Ahh, you must be one of those eagle-eyed readers on a budget trying to Lean FIRE. Or you just like to make it hard for me to sell my guru wares that promise an exotic no-day-job lifestyle. Either way, I suppose it's important to not gloss over this.

In order to help illustrate the concepts in this book, let's have a little fun and create a pretend person to act as our puppet. Let's call him Lenny the Landlord. Lenny is going to be our guinea pig for the rest of the book, and we're going to put him through his paces. We'll make him rich and bring him to the brink of financial ruin, and he'll thank us for it, you'll see.

So let's consider Lenny for a moment. Lenny is forty, single, and he's got $100,000 to invest. Maybe it's cash, maybe it's in an IRA, or maybe it's locked up in equity in his personal home that he can access with a home equity line of credit. Doesn't matter, he's sitting on $100,000. And he thinks stocks are safe, so he invests for himself online in a variety of self-taught options via an online brokerage.

Lenny makes these willy-nilly purchases without a licensed advisor telling him if his stock pick makes sense for his retirement plans. No one is looking at Lenny's personal bank balances and current income and outstanding debts to confirm if spending $100,000 is the most prudent thing for him to be doing with his money. Lenny can spend a hundred grand on stocks unsupervised and unaided with very little effort, and if the investment goes south, well, shit happens, as Lenny likes to say to explain away this ignorance.

Oh, but Lenny has learned and wants to invest in real estate now and has been binge watching Dave Ramsey videos and thinks mortgages are the work of the devil.

Lenny wants to spend his one hundred large on real estate. He finds an off-market property with a tenant, and to reduce risk he buys this property in cash. And he saves money without using a real estate agent since he has a direct connection to the seller. This behavior is actually the exact same risk as buying in stocks. Lenny has no guidance, no safety net, and he is actually creating risk buying houses this way, not reducing it.

So what is the safest way for Lenny to buy real estate? Easy. He should buy as many homes with mortgages as he can. Thanks to laws enacted from the 2009 post–real estate crash, buying a rental property with a fixed-rate mortgage is the safest investing one can possibly do. Not only that, he should use a real estate agent. Buyers don't pay real estate agents; sellers of properties pay both agents, so they are free for Lenny to use. Look at all the safety nets Lenny gets if he buys property this way:

- A real estate agent confirming value of property and free expert advice on neighborhood amenities and local trends.

- Time to conduct a home inspection on the property confirming Lenny knows every possible thing about what he is about to buy.

- A nosy mortgage lender sniffing around every financial document Lenny has confirming this will not be a risky investment for him and that he can actually afford it.

- An independent third-party appraisal required by the mortgage lender confirming the value of the property matches the value in the contract.

- A reduced buy-in on the asset. Lenny only has to spend $25,000 to acquire a $100,000 asset using a 25% down payment. If a bank, the most conservative money-lending institution around, approves Lenny for a loan, they are effectively stating they are willing to partner with him on it for the remaining $75,000 and take on 75% of the remaining risk. In essence, the ol' stodgy bank will give you money as they have deemed it a very safe investment.

Okay, so that convoluted process and the trouble you have to go through in buying real estate actually reduces risk, huh? Pretty cool, right? I'll give you more examples later in the book about why a mortgage is an amazing tool. And I mean a real tool, like a rigid bar resting on a pivot used to help move a heavy load. Such a tool is referred to as a lever. And we know a lever creates leverage. Maybe we can use leverage to move some heavy bags of riches into your early retirement plans.

I like where this is going. And if you are highlighting important parts of this book, this next sentence is for you to make it glow in magnificent fluorescence. The safest investing approach is using leverage, and thus, leverage is going to be the most important tool in reaching House FIRE.

So maybe Lenny doesn't really understand the leverage concept yet and he feels like he would simply make more money by going out and buying a single $100,000 rental property and have no mortgage at all. Lenny could find a real winner that he can then rent out for, say, $1,250 per month, or $15,000 a year. He'll have to budget for maintenance and other costs, so let's say that when it's all said and done, Lenny's single home earns him $10,000 per year in positive cash flow (his income minus all expenses), or a nice 10% return on his investment, right?

Not bad. But what happens when the home is vacant? Suppose Lenny's tenants move out and his house sits empty for a month. Well, he's still on the hook for property taxes, insurance, and so on. Also, although Lenny can depreciate the house—that's one of the great IRS real estate tax advantages—he's still got a tax bill to pay every year on the income.

Here's a basic and rounded off look at Lenny's tax bill. We'll assume a 30% tax bracket:

- $10,000 annual net income
- $3,000 depreciation write-off (a tax benefit for real estate investors based on home value)
- $7,000 net taxable passive income ($10,000 minus $3,000 from the numbers above)
- $2,100 taxes owed (30% tax on $7,000)
- $7,900 annual after-tax income ($10,000 annual net income minus $2,100 taxes owed)

So Lenny's 10% ROI (return on investment) is now down to 7.9% ($7,900 after-tax income/$100,000 invested). Still not bad, though. Dave Ramsey would still approve. Except for that month with no income, which then lowers the return to about 7.1% or so. That's about the same for what he'd get in the stock market in an average year.

Now, what would happen if Lenny took his $100K and bought four houses? He buys four $100K homes, putting $25K down for each one. They all rent for the same $1,250, and they all make $10K per year after internal expenses.

Well, you say, Lenny has to pay a mortgage on each property. Fair enough. Let's say that each mortgage costs him $5,000 per year ($75,000 mortgage at 5% interest is about $415 a month). Here's a quick snapshot:

- $40,000 annual gross income made payable to Lenny the Landlord
- $20,000 debt service paid payable to Devil Mortgage Company
- $20,000 positive cash flow to a happy Lenny

Hmm, it already looks like Lenny is making more money with four units. And even if one sits vacant for a month, it's only a quarter of his monthly income, not 100%. Think of it as Lenny sitting in a rowboat. In the first example, if he stops rowing, the boat comes to a stop. In the second example, he's got four guys rowing, so if one stops, the boat only slows a little bit.

But what about the taxes? If Lenny has to pay $2,100 on one property, then surely he has to pay $8,400 on four. Wouldn't that reduce his return to less than 5%?

Nope. Watch this:

- $40,000 net annual income
- $12,000 depreciation tax write-off
- $12,000 mortgage interest deduction
- $16,000 net taxable income
- $11,200 annual after-tax income ($16,000 annual net income minus $4,800 taxes owed)

At 30% tax rate, Lenny only has to pay the IRS $4,800 per year, leaving him with an actual after-tax cash-on-cash return of $11,200 per year or 11.2%.

Tah-dah! By leveraging the properties, Lenny not only reduces his risk, he also takes advantage of more tax deductions and increases his overall ROI to over 10%. Now that's the power of leveraging real estate, my friend. And Lenny already has four properties to really set him up for the House FIRE life.

Oh, not convinced are ye? Well, let me strike the expired equine with even greater force.

Let's skip ahead five years and compare Lenny's two scenarios. We're going to make three assumptions: first, that he increases rent by $25 every year; second, his fixed mortgage payments are paying down his mortgage by a conservative 3% annually; and third, that his properties are appreciating by a conservative 3% each year as well.

In scenario one, after only five years, this is what Lenny's situation looks like with his one paid-off rental house that he bought in all cash with Dave Ramsey's blessing:

Note: These are rounded annual numbers for illustration only.

- Down payment: $100,000
- Home value: $115,000
- Total equity: $115,000
- Gross rental income: $16,800
- Internal expenses (repairs, maintenance, taxes, insurance, etc.): $5,000
- Net rental income: $11,800
- Depreciation deduction: $3,000 (based on original purchase price)

- Net taxable income: $8,800
- Taxes owed: $2,640
- Total after-tax ROI (Net income - Taxes/Down payment): $9,160/9.16%

Okay, not bad? After five years, Lenny has brought his total after-tax cash-on-cash return to 9.16%, which is pretty good. Now let's look at scenario 2 where Lenny bought four houses with the same $100,000 that he leveraged with my blessing and how they shape up five years later:

- Four home total value: $460,000
- Total loan owed: $275,000 (after five years of principal paydown)
- Total equity: $185,000
- Gross rental income: $67,200 ($16,800 x 4 homes)
- Internal expenses: $20,000 ($5,000 x 4 homes)
- Net rental income: $47,200
- Depreciation deduction: $12,000 (based on original purchase price)
- Mortgage interest deduction: $12,000
- Net taxable income: $23,200
- Taxes owed: $6,960
- Debt service (mortgage payments): $20,000 ($415 a month x 4 homes)
- Total after-tax ROI (Net income - Debt service - Taxes/Down payment): $20,240/20.2%

Once again, Lenny is ahead with four leveraged homes, isn't he? Not only is his cash-on-cash return over 20% after taxes, he's also got $70,000 more in equity in those four houses as opposed to the single home he bought with cash. That's because he uses the real estate investor's best friend—the bank—who takes 75% of the risk and lets Lenny keep 100% of the reward.

With $100,000 to start and five years in the real estate market, he's almost achieved Lean FIRE with $20,000 a year in living expenses covered. Imagine if he had five properties? Or if he did this over ten years? Or if he raised rent by $50 one year instead of just $25?

Isn't it better to have four units than just one? A bigger portfolio means bigger opportunities. And let's not forget bigger passive income. Now getting to this type of passive income is what I'm going to teach you to live off, not some huge savings account. It's much more profitable, and more fun, this way.

Although your first few properties are going to be anything but "passive" in the true sense, it's the IRS's definition of passive that we're talking about. Passive income is any income you derive from assets where you don't have a day-to-day—or job-like—involvement in the creation of the income. This is how landlords make money in their sleep and get rich dreaming.

Some other examples of passive income include these:

- Royalties from a book you wrote or song you recorded
- YouTube videos that have monetized commercials
- Interest payments on money you lend
- Dividend stocks
- Affiliate marketing links on your website
- Licensing your intellectual property or patents
- Online courses you sell (videos, instruction manuals, downloadable spreadsheets)

Passive is the best because all you have to pay is income tax and you also don't have to punch a clock to get it. Yes, for real estate you'll have to meet tenants and take applications and probably fix a toilet or two, but that stuff doesn't happen every day, so the rent you collect is still mainly passive. And passive income is the very best way to create, preserve, and grow your wealth.

Just like recording a song you can license or making a popular monetized YouTube video, you have to work hard up front to get those perpetual greenbacks to passively hit your bank account in the future. But as your portfolio grows up to your first few properties in real estate, you'll see that there are ways to remove yourself even from the few tasks that are required to manage your properties, and then you are really going to see green.

Yes, there are people called property managers who do all the management stuff you don't want to do to make this so lazy, even Lenny the Landlord could do it. Oh, by the way, real estate is also the best asset you can pass on to your children or grandchildren too.

Easiest Way to Create Generational Wealth

Let's talk for a quick second about *wealth* and what that word really means. Wealth, as defined by Robert Kiyosaki's *Rich Dad, Poor Dad* book, is the number of days you can go without working and still pay your bills.

So, for example, if Lenny has monthly expenses of $5,000 and he's got $2,500 in the bank, then he has fifteen days of wealth. On the other hand, if Lenny's real estate portfolio produces an after-tax cash flow of $5,000 or more per month, then Lenny has infinite wealth. He's financially free. He has House FIRE'd. And the longer he holds that portfolio of homes, the more income he will generate from it.

Now, when it comes to wealth, consider these three pieces: the creation of wealth, the growth of wealth, and the preservation of wealth. All three are important and guess what? Real estate lets you do all three very well.

For example, Lenny previously bought four houses that give him an annual after-tax return of $10,800. He's created some wealth, right? Now, with each passing year or with each new tenant, Lenny is growing his wealth in three ways:

- He's paying down his mortgage and increasing his equity in each property.

- He's increasing rents and therefore increasing his cash flow.

- His properties may be appreciating in value and thereby increasing his equity further.

And Lenny's wealth is protected by a physical asset that gives him tax advantages. Lenny can even pass these four houses off to his kids one day, too, and do it in such a way that they get all the benefits of this wealth without incurring any taxes.

How that's done is a bit complex, and I won't get into it now. However, just remember that the IRS really appreciates real estate investors and gives us a lot of ways to create, grow, and preserve our wealth. Why? Because it's good for the economy and good for the culture. Landlords provide places for people to live, and rental property also generates taxable income. Occupied homes, be they owner-occupied or rented, help to promote a strong and stable economy.

So with real estate, you don't need a bunch of college degrees and you don't need big connections or family wealth to create, grow, and preserve your wealth—and to pass it on to the next generation. First, understand both of my parents were teachers. My grandparents were teachers. I'm from an education first family.

But guess what, fancy degrees are the opposite of passive income and growing wealth quickly. If you study to be a medical doctor, how do you make money in your sleep? You still have to show up in person each day and evaluate patients. If you get a law degree, how does your education passively grow into an asset you can sell or pass down to your kids one day? If you get any highfalutin degrees, you are empowering yourself to earn a higher income, yes, but you actively have to be there to earn that income. Nothing wrong with that. But there are only so many hours in a day you can work.

You will have difficulty scaling your high-demand skill set without opening your own business. And that's the beauty of real estate. It's opening your own small business with no license needed to operate. And no sleepless nights cramming for a state-mandated test. And no student loans to pay off once you get started. And no brick-and-mortar office with a fancy sign needed either. Idiots like me run rampant in the real estate world, and, well, so you really have no excuse. You just need a mindset that you can do it too.

So why haven't you bought real estate yet? I probably know why.

Watch Out for Well-meaning Advice

Okay, this is a bit of a departure, but I think it needs to be said. Have you ever heard of the "crabs in a bucket" syndrome? Basically, if you put a few crabs into a bucket, some interesting behaviors show up. For one, you'd think that a crab could climb out of the top of the bucket, especially if there is no lid.

You're right too. They *can* but they *don't*. The reason is simple: when a crab begins to climb out, the other crabs will grab it and pull it back down. It's a weird phenomenon but hardly unique to crabs. We silly humans do it too.

What I'm trying to say here is that when you decide to launch your real estate career, you're probably going to want to tell all of your friends, family, and coworkers. Inevitably, most of them will tell you that it's a bad idea. They'll say real estate is too risky, it's too hard, it costs too much money, the time isn't right—or the best one of all: well, I tried it and it didn't work.

If that's so, then how come so many people do it? I'll bet you know of at least one person who isn't particularly bright or brilliant who's made money in real estate. (Hint, you are reading his book.) Yet all of your well-meaning crabs will try to save you from making a big imaginary mistake and pull you back down into the bucket with them.

The truth is that real estate investing, unlike many other types of investing, does have a steep learning curve. There's a lot to know if you want to be successful. And invariably, the people who don't succeed try to avoid the learning process and therefore fail because they really don't know what to do or how to do it right. I've actually developed a working model for this called the Real Estate Investing Flywheel, which I'll discuss in a later chapter.

The point is this: don't let Debbie Downers derail your investing career and your path to FIRE. Don't take advice from people who have never actually *done* something. Or from folks who tried it once without any knowledge or preparation and failed. Most landlords with bad experiences inherited their properties and were reluctant investors and thus unprepared. Take my advice—get your advice from those who have successfully walked the FIRE path you want to walk.

But do you want to know what's really risky? Doing nothing. Missing out on thousands in passive cash flow. Missing out on potentially millions in net worth from tenants paying down mortgages while you are increasing rents. Missing out on true and lasting financial freedom from that dreary job where dreary people do dreary tasks in order to maintain their dreary lives. You are missing out on gold-leafing bald eagle eggs.

Missing out is not for me and it's not for you. House FIRE is your best way to never miss out on anything ever.

You're Becoming a Multi-entrepreneur

Before we move on to greener pastures, I'd like to expand on my earlier point of something regarding real estate. When you become an investor, you're actually becoming an entrepreneur. Even more than that, each property that you buy is in truth its own small business.

Think about it. Every house has income, expenses, and profit. Sure, each one might only throw off $100 per month in profit at first, but you have to start somewhere, right?

The beauty of this approach is that each of these little businesses has the same opportunity for growth and prosperity as any type of business.

- You can increase rents over time to increase the profits.
- You can pay off any debt to increase the equity.
- You can shop for cheaper home insurance to cut costs.
- You can make improvements and increase the perceived value and increase your equity.
- You can even refinance after a while, pull out your initial capital, and then any cash thrown off after that is pure and infinite profit.

Wait, what is infinite profit? That sounds like something to understand. A real quick example with Lenny. He still has $100,000 burning a hole in his pocket. He buys a house for

$150,000 with 25% down, so he spends $37,500 of it for down payment and gets a $112,500 mortgage for the rest. Lenny also negotiates for the seller to pay the closing costs on the purchase of about $5,000 so he doesn't have to budget for that. When it is all said and done, Lenny has monthly payments of $625. He then spends $62,500 fixing up the house—maybe he adds a master bedroom and bathroom suite off the back and does cosmetic updates inside. And maybe he pulls a Chip and JoJo and goes nuts with shiplap. It doesn't matter, he makes the house better.

When done, the home is valued at a new price of $284,000, a $134,000 improvement. So he refinances it at a bank, which will only loan him 75% of the ARV (after-rehab value) of the home. A new mortgage is then signed for $213,000. This pays off his previous mortgage of $112,500 and he gets the difference in the form of a check at closing for some of the remaining equity in the home of $100,500. And now he has a much bigger $1,200 a month mortgage payment to worry about.

So he paid $100,000 to buy and renovate an entire home and he got back $100,500 tax-free since he didn't sell the property. That only sounds like a $500 profit right? Not the wisest investment for Lenny, you may say? And on top of that his mortgage payment doubled. Now you yell at Lenny and call him another idiot just dreaming of starting his own HGTV career.

Hold up, my budding chefs. This is an amazing investment. He still has a house with $71,000 of equity in it if he chooses to put it on the market to sell (the 25% of ARV of the home the bank made him keep invested in it). He can also rent it out for $1,500 a month now since it's new and shiny. So he basically has a free rental house as he got all the money back he put into it plus a $500 kicker.

Before	After
Before	**After**
House Value at Purchase: $150,000	House ARV (after-rehab value): $284,000
25% Down Payment: $37,500	25% Equity Value in Home: $71,000
Mortgage Balance: $112,500	Mortgage Balance: $213,000
Monthly Loan Payment: $625	Monthly Loan Payment: $1,200
Renovation Cost: $62,500	New Rental Amount: $1,500
Total Lenny Cash Needed: $100,000	Cash-out Check to Lenny: $100,500

The tenants help Lenny build even more equity each month with each rent payment, which pays down the principal some and Lenny gets to pocket the $300 cash flow overage. There shouldn't be many repairs for a while either since he just renovated everything.

Now this is how you get infinite returns on his $0 he currently has invested in this home. Even if the bank forecloses on this home because Lenny all of a sudden has amazing ineptitude and never makes a mortgage payment, he loses no money in the investment since he already has all his money back. Hmm, actually that's pretty smart to build a zero-risk safety net in a rental house this way. I think you owe Lenny an apology.

This move is one of the most important keys to long-term and big-time real estate investing success. You purchase assets, exit your cash tax-free, and still keep the money-making assets. That's the magic of real estate to help you expediate your way to HELLFIRE. This is only one way to walk along the House FIRE path. I will cover more in later chapters, don't fret.

Now that you've seen a few good reasons to invest in real estate, let's take a look at the true focus of this book. In the next chapter, I'll explain why I think you can really change your life with just a few properties and the importance of your first couple rentals in order to set you on the path to whatever financial goals you desire and how the Real Estate Investing Flywheel will make it all happen for you.

Maybe you a just want one rental, and that's fine. It will still help you financially. But, like anything, the more you scale your investments, the more return you'll get. Moving forward I'm going to talk about reaching five rental properties. You'll see in due time why five is the magic number to House FIRE. But listen, keep reading if you just want one. One property will help, but five is true financial independence.

So now the good stuff is coming, or what Gordon Ramsay calls the protein portion of a well-balanced real estate meal. I'll chill out on the Gordon Ramsay analogy after this, it's making me hungry.

3

"Alan, five properties sounds like I'm lighting a blaze. I just want one small spark."

Why did I choose five properties as the most scalable point of reaching House FIRE (to be financially independent and retire early)? Is there a reason for that number or did I just choose it randomly?

The truth is that I was drunk off boxed wine and it seemed like a good idea at the time. No, not really, I was drunk off whiskey. However, there is a strong reason why this book is now going to focus not just on your first property, but on your first five properties.

When I first got into real estate investing, I set a goal to buy five properties in five years. Why? I really didn't like corporate life and thought after five years I would go crazy remaining in that type of environment. So I went to work on an exit plan. One property per year. Could I do that?

At the time, I thought that five properties in five years was a crazy goal, especially on an average salary in one of the most expensive cities in the world. But I needed to attain that goal. It wasn't a choice.

I really wanted to exit the corporate world and, well, live life for myself. I wanted to stop setting the alarm clock to wake up early to increase someone else's wealth. I wanted to stop checking my phone to help make someone else rich. So I set this goal and I stuck to it. That's something I learned early on—set a goal and stick to it, no matter what it takes. Force yourself or even trick yourself into meeting the goal. Or treat it as the only goal, and nothing else will stop you.

Now it's entirely possible to get your first five properties in a single year if you want to, but then you are probably a speed reader and have already gotten to the end of this book and you are reading it for the fifth time. This is my book, so let me be the overachiever for now, please. Geez, some people just gotta be show-offs.

Back to goal setting. It's boring, right? Every self-help book or how-to book blathers on about setting goals and reaching goals and setting new goals ad nauseum, it seems. Of course there must be a reason. It's true. If you don't set and then take actions to meet your goals, the odds that you'll actually attain what you want goes down by several orders of magnitude. Ding ding!

Like NY Yankee Yogi Berra's motivational quote: "If you don't know where you are going, you'll end up someplace else." Makes sense, right? Figure out if you want to replace your day job income, or if you want to support your weird hobby, or if you just want to have internet for life. I don't care why you are doing this, but you should care.

Now I'm not going to spend too much time on this. There are lots of great books on goal setting and most of us now understand this concept and the psychology behind it. However, I will say just a few words.

I'll assume you know nothing about real estate and don't know what you are capable of. So I will set your first goal for you. Your first goal is that you will buy your first house within three months from today. It's something you can actually achieve without monumental effort. This book is all you need. And then you can decide if you want more properties after that.

But look at the day and make note of when you are reading this sentence. In three months or less you will own a property. And let me know @TheHouseOfAC on any social media channel so I can relish in the moment with you.

Like I said, my goal at first was to buy a rental house each year for five years to have cash flow replace all my monthly bills. That's an easy goal, to be honest, as I wasn't making a ton of money at my day job and didn't have a ton of expenses. But if you just want to buy one or two homes, that's fine too. If you want only one house to pay for your Tesla payment, then go for it. I have a hunch after the first one you'll see the light, the FIRE light, and want to buy a few more properties to improve your quality of life a little bit more.

However, what you don't want to do, at least not yet, is set a goal to buy one house every month. Believe me, that *is* possible, but it's hard when you're just getting started. Real estate is a get-rich-slowly type of venture and speed-purchasing investments isn't really a shortcut to riches.

My advice? After you buy your first house in three months, try to buy one house every twelve months after that. That gives you plenty of time to look at properties, talk to sellers, analyze deals, and make offers as well as to give yourself plenty of time to get any financing in order. I recommend one house per year only because it allows you time to be conscientious and learn as you go.

You can move faster if you desire, naturally, but this is a good pace at which to start. No matter what, though, I strongly recommend that you start looking for your next house right after each closing.

Yet even at this modest schedule, I still became a millionaire from the purchase of those first five houses. A net worth millionaire, to be clear, not a cash-flowing millionaire. But I did reach my goal of having all expenses being covered. Yet it's still an incredible feat for a young guy to achieve before he turned thirty. You can do it at any age.

Here's what's really cool. Before I started investing in real estate, I had a net worth of $10,000. By the time I bought five properties and owned the fifth one for a year, I'd grown my net worth into just over a million dollars. That's significant when you consider I could officially FIRE at the age of twenty-eight.

Traditional FIRE would have had me work an extra five to ten years and save an extra $250,000 to hit my FIRE number and move most of my investments to mutual funds, but then my life would be the exact same for the rest of my life. I would be on a budget. I would not be able to increase my lifestyle spend each year if I wanted to. I wouldn't be able to splurge. I wouldn't be able to talk trash to a gray discount big box store.

But now, I had options. I chose to use the equity in those first five homes to get my next five, and I can tell you that properties five through ten came very fast and carried far more profit.

Now I'm not suggesting that you will end up with a million in net worth after you buy your fifth property. Part of my success was that I got lucky as well as smart. I'm not expecting you to make a million with your first five, and you shouldn't expect those results either. Yet given enough time, it will happen. This will be a get-rich-slow game, no matter what, and luck is really the only accelerator to riches.

But owning five properties gets you five imaginary lottery tickets to potential rapid home appreciation, which happened to me. I didn't know Brooklyn would become the next big thing. I bought for the rental income, and the appreciation was an unexpected surprise. I'll cover that in a bit, but for now, let's keep it more realistic and set our expectations around acquiring a property in three months. If you exceed it, great.

Kill the Bills

This is the main mindset you need to House FIRE so it's worth going into detail a little more. Each new house you buy is not going to make you rich. Your average single family home with 80% leverage will probably make you $120 to $200 per month in positive cash flow. Aside from the debt service, you have to factor in maintenance, vacancy, and management costs—even if that's you. Your home might have a lawn or pool service and so on. It's like I mentioned in the previous chapter, each house is more like a small business that makes you $1,500 to $2,400 a year in cash flow.

Yet with five properties, it certainly gets better, doesn't it? And as time goes on, as you saw with Lenny, rents go up, expenses go down, and your cash flow as well as net worth go up. Yet in order to keep things grounded and realistic, here's how I see each new house.

Each new home I bought when I was going after my first five was a way to pay a bill. It's one of the secrets of the rich and a smart strategy to get you to FIRE. Here's what I mean:

Job people decide to buy a boat that costs $50,000 and then go to the bank and get a loan that they have to pay on each month with interest. So every month, the boat decreases their spendable income by $1,000, let's say, their monthly boat payment. Eventually the boat will be paid off. Now here's what Lenny the Landlord does as a savvy rich guy. Lenny says, "Okay, I want a boat that's going to cost me $1,000 each month, so in order to pay for it, I need to go find a property or two or three that throw off $1,000 per month in after-tax cash flow."

That's one of the biggest secrets of the wealthy. They don't borrow money to buy boats and cars and RVs and stuff; they borrow money to buy an asset that generates income that pays for those toys. Lenny effectively gets a free boat this way—and eventually a free rental property when his tenants pay off the mortgage over time. And by then, the boat will be paid off too. Anyone else want a free boat?

This doesn't just apply to big purchases like boats or RVs. You can do it with even the smaller bills like I did—for example, that $150 internet bill that I was paying every month that made Costco whimper in the corner.

Then I did the same thing for my cell phone bill, my electric bill, my gas and water bills, grocery costs, and monthly subway pass. By the time I had four houses, all of my auxiliary monthly bills were paid for by rental income. I wasn't out of the rat race, as they say, but really close. And such reduced expenses helped me quickly save for my fifth property.

When I went on to my fifth property, I actually was able to get myself free of the daily 9-to-5 grind as that rental income was used to pursue new ventures. That is reaching House FIRE, and it's a feeling like none other.

Remember that buying your first five properties isn't a get-rich-quick scheme. It took me seven years with a lot of luck, but if you have a ten- to fifteen-year horizon, then that's easy breezy. It's about establishing a foundation for future success. It's about acquiring profitable properties in any market. You are giving yourself options: options to leave your day job, options to pursue a hobby, options to do bigger and more profitable investing. What value do you put on these options you never had before?

I want to pause for a second and explain something.

When I say first five properties, I don't necessarily mean single family homes. Real estate investing is a broad concept and covers a lot of different types of property and different ways to make money. This book focuses primarily on rentals, yet that's hardly your only option.

Even with rentals, though, you're not limited to single family homes. Think about it. Residential rentals cover everything from mobile homes to multifamily properties like duplexes up to huge apartment complexes.

If you can make $500 from five houses, what would happen if you bought five duplexes? A duplex costs the same as any single family home its size, and yet it offers you two units instead of one. Yes, each unit will rent for less than a single family home of the same size, but there are two of them.

Consider this: Lenny buys himself a 2,000-square-foot house and a 2,000-square-foot duplex. The house rents for $1,500 per month. The duplex is divided into two two-bedroom, two-bath units. Each unit rents for $900 per month. With the duplex, Lenny has $1,800 of monthly rental income.

Both properties cost the same, yet the duplex generates more income. Imagine if your first five properties were all duplexes. Now maybe each one makes you $200 per month. So $1,000 per month certainly changes the game, doesn't it?

In many parts of the country there are also triplexes and even fourplexes. Generally any multifamily property up to four units is treated just like a single family home by mortgage lenders. So keep this in mind. You're not limited to single family homes. You're not even limited to only one type of rental property.

Don't Go for Perfection

Okay, this is a point that I can't stress enough. So many times, I've worked with investors who forget this. They look at each property as their personal property and want it to reflect what they'd like their own home to be.

Please keep in mind: you're an investor. You aren't buying your dream home or even properties you'd like to live in. You're purchasing an asset that generates income. It needs to be good enough for the type of tenant who will rent it, not necessarily for you.

In fact, I'll go further and state that your first property will probably be anything but perfect. It might need a little work, or be in an area of town you might not choose to live. We're not going for perfection here. What we're aiming for is good enough.

I've got a friend and fellow investor whom I coached a few years back. She now has purchased her third property, and you'd think that she knows her business by now.

Well, she does, yet I was talking with her right after a recent purchase. She wanted me to come over and check out her new acquisition. It was a modest 3/2 home of about 1,700 square feet. When I arrived, I saw some intense construction going on. I saw Angela standing in the front room watching men tear up the ceiling and cut away at the roof supports.

"What's up?" I asked, curious. "Got some damage?"

"No," she said with a big grin on her face. "I'm having a vaulted ceiling put in."

I asked her why and she said that it would look nice. I asked how much she was spending and she said $10,000. Then I asked about how this would affect her rent.

"Well," Angela said, "I'm already going to charge $1,300 for this place, which is about the max in this neighborhood, so I won't be able to raise it anymore."

"So this $10K renovation isn't going to increase the revenue?" I asked in confusion. "Then why are you doing it?"

"Because I like vaulted ceilings" was her response.

I couldn't believe it. Angela was basically throwing away the next three years of profits on that house simply because *she* liked vaulted ceilings, even though *she* wasn't even living in the house.

Please don't fall into this trap. Never forget that you're buying a business and a business needs to be profitable. You aren't going to be accused of being a slumlord because you didn't upgrade the ceiling heights. You can provide a place you and the tenant are proud to live in with reasonable renovations. Plus I've found many tenants don't want a vaulted ceiling—it's just more space they have to pay to heat and cool, which runs up their utility bills. And that can make it harder for them to pay you their rent money.

Angela learned from this investing hiccup thankfully and is killing it on her path of House FIRE now.

Listen, you're going to be an Angela at times and make mistakes too. Think about it. Have you ever started something new and had nothing ever go wrong or make the perfect decision at every crossroads? Of course not. That's part of the learning process. I still make bonehead decisions and have been known to hire the wrong contractor or obscenely underestimate repair costs. Sometimes I lose money on a house.

The key is to persevere and learn from your mistakes and from the obstacles you'll have to overcome. This cycle is almost like maybe a flywheel that is gaining momentum and gets faster and more efficient over time. Nah, that can't be it. That's a terrible analogy. I'll try to think of another one.

In short, just don't make your life any harder than it has to be by losing your perspective. Create a goal, act on that goal, and then learn from your mistakes that next time you do it. Don't beat yourself up about a poor decision.

A lot of things will go through your mind as you begin your real estate investing career. You'll get nervous, excited, broke, rich, overwhelmed, too involved, not involved enough, exhausted, and energized. It's natural and part of the learning and growing process. But see, that's maybe more important and will make you more successful than the actual five properties themselves. Because, as with all success, it's the strength you develop that really makes it happen.

When Is the Best Time to Start?

This is the most common question I get from folks who want to start investing in real estate. It's a natural one, after all.

- Should I wait until I have a bigger down payment?
- Should I wait for interest rates to drop?
- Should I wait until the kids are off to school?
- Should I wait until *I'm* done with school?

Well, I do have the answer and it's actually quite simple: the best time to invest in real estate is two years ago when you asked me the first time! So many people read the books, ask me all the questions in this book, and then do nothing but use my book cover to tie the room together.

I say that because, as an investor who has personally coached others, this dilemma comes up a lot. The real answer, though, is even simpler. The best time to start investing in real estate is *right now*! You start right now, you'll have your first home in three months.

But, Alan, you might say, prices are high, the market is uncertain—

Maybe you've been reading about real estate for years now. Maybe this has been a dream for decades. Maybe you have been sitting on that inheritance for three years paralyzed what to do with it. Maybe you are only two and half chapters into even considering anything related to real estate, and, well, good timing on your end.

The fact is that you can be successful in real estate investing in any market and in any economic climate. It's true. Waiting to start is the worst thing you can do. For instance, consider these circumstances:

- If home prices are really high and going up, then you can buy, fix, and resell a property for profit. If the numbers work to rent out now, it will still work when prices go up.

- If home prices are low and dropping quickly, then you can buy a property to rent now and fix up later. A lease will have a twelve-month lag time on price correction, but rarely do rental prices go down much; it's just the price of the house that goes down.

- If the country is in a recession, then you can buy a rental unit or an apartment building at a discount. No recession is going to last forever. But if your property is making money in a recession, then it will make more money in the recovery.

- If the country is in a strong growth period, then you can buy rentals or flips or sell the properties you acquired in a down market. If you have more than one, then you can try to time the market. But I've found it's best to keep the property in high times and refinance them to pull your cash out. Then you can acquire more properties.

- If the country is in a global pandemic, well I have found opportunities to both buy low and sell high as everyone is being affected differently. Some buyers must have an outdoor space and a pool and will pay extra for it. Some can't find steady work and are willing to sell their house with a pool at a discount. Unusual occurrences will have unusual opportunities depending if you want to buy or sell.

As long as the numbers work, you can invest in real estate. And numbers can work in any market. It's important that you accurately analyze a property, be it a fix and flip or a rental or a fix and rent or whatever. And I'll explain how to do all this, and I'll make it stupid easy for you.

But if you are holding rentals long term, it really doesn't matter what is happening in the market. If you bought at the worst time possible, say 2008 to 2009, it would take seven years for your property to regain its value if you wanted to sell it again and not lose money. And that's having the worst timing possible. You would still have had no issue finding a renter during those seven years and you'd still easily be profitable—as long as you got a fixed-rate mortgage instead of a variable-rate mortgage, which was the downfall of many homeowners during that time period.

In short, a learning experience is just as valuable as a solid dollar, after all. And when home prices drop, it doesn't always mean rental prices drop too. I'm not suggesting you go about it willy-nilly. Don't intentionally make a huge mistake. But if you do or your returns aren't as high as you thought when you bought that first house, it's okay. You'll learn and grow and all that wisdom stacks onto each new property. And the market will eventually turn, which makes the true riches come the longer you are in the game.

On the other hand, you may have missed out on some awesome opportunities because you waited. The only perfect vision, the only 100% accurate predictions, comes from hindsight. You just can't know the future, so why worry about it? Don't wait until "the time is right" because guess what, Grasshopper, it never is—at least if you think of it as the perfect time.

And here is a nugget of info for you, more head-scratching House FIRE advice that goes against the grain. If you raise your rent each year, it makes your tenants stay longer. Say what, Buttercup?

That's right. If you raise your rent annually, your tenants will want to stay. Let's watch Lenny in action on this seemingly upside-down logic.

Lenny the Landlord's motivation is to keep his properties fully occupied and to get market rent or higher on each of his rental units. Tina the Tenant's motivation is to have a stable and reliable place of shelter and pay market rent or below wherever she chooses to stay. So how do they meet in the middle? Well, the sweet spot is obviously paying as close to market rent as possible as both sides are okay with that.

If Lenny rents his home out for $1,000 a month to Tina to start, that's market rent and both sides are happy on move-in day. Lenny the Landlord stays pretty cool keeping Tina the Tenant around over five years by continuing to charge $1,000 a month. It's a nice and reliable safe spot and things are pretty consistent.

Now landlord expenses creep up a little each year— insurance, taxes, and so on. So by not raising rent for five years, Lenny will eventually be losing money and not killing any bills with this property. He's going to have to make a change or he extinguishes his FIRE.

A real estate agent Lenny knows swings by and says market rent is $1,250 now if it was vacant, and, well, Lenny goes to Tina and says, "Hey, I've been cool for the last five years, but you've got to prepare for a $250 bump in rent. It's just a $3,000 annual increase for you so I can break even on my property."

Tina yells at Lenny for being greedy and notifies him immediately with her two middle fingers that she is moving out. And she may trash the place on the way out. Tina, like most humans, didn't spend the last four years saving the difference between what she was paying in rent and what she should have been paying in rent. No human does that.

Now let's play out this scenario in an alternative universe. If instead Lenny raised the rent $50 each year, that would be a $600 bump on Tina's expenses come lease renewal each year. Tina figures it would cost her about $600 to move—she would have to take off work, rent a moving truck, maybe get new furniture, might have a longer commute to work that adds to her gas bill, and all kinds of other scenarios.

Tina decides to stay and be cool with the slight bump in rent. Plus she likes the house, it's her home and it's comforting, and she likes the community within the neighborhood. If Lenny does this same $50 bump each year, Tina will continue to stay. She has the same process. To her, staying is the same cost as moving without the effort. And she's happy where she is.

We keep this up, and by year five, Lenny is only charging Tina $1,200 with his incremental bumps instead of the $1,250 market rate like the real estate agent suggested it is worth. Now Tina is thrilled to stay, because it is the same cost as moving, and she is paying under market rent. She is saving $600 by staying. Win-win for Tina and a win-win for Lenny. Lenny avoided not only a vacancy by raising rent, but also double birds from Tina. #LandlordGoals.

So I got sidetracked a bit with that Lenny anecdote. The important thing is that all markets are a good market to buy in. All markets are a good time to rent out in. And you can do other real estate deals like flips and renovations when market conditions present themselves. So the right time is now for you to buy, and if you start now, you'll earn your Landlord name in the next three months. That will always be true.

For the history buffs out there, here's a quick story. It was the eve of a great battle and one of Napoleon's advisors came to him and said that the enemy outnumbered them. The weather wasn't quite right as well. He advised that they wait until conditions were right. Napoleon looked up from his maps and into the young man's eyes and said: "Conditions, hell! I *make* conditions! We attack *now!*"

In the next chapter, I'm finally going to dive into my model for the perfect investor so, like Napoleon, you can attack now. You are the little engine that could, and you will make your FIRE dreams come true.

4

"Alan, I don't get how flies on wheels has anything to do with lighting up my future."

Here we are at the very heart, the crux of this book—a little invention I modestly call The House of AC (Alan Corey) Hyper Accurate Ultra-unique Real Estate Investing Flywheel of Success, Riches, and Happiness.

Okay, it's just the REI Flywheel. It's actually a simple but effective way to look at your real estate investing career. To understand the REI Flywheel, you just need a journeyman's understanding of calculus, a complete mastery of the entire chronology of human development, and a PhD in applied quantum physics. It couldn't be easier.

All kidding aside, though, the Real Estate Investing Flywheel is a way for you to visualize your investing efforts and something to which you can refer and keep track of your progress. The flywheel applies to every stage of your investing, from the day you begin thinking about your first property to the day you close on that 500-unit apartment complex and beyond.

First, understand that a flywheel is a heavy wheel that takes tremendous force to get cranking. Eventually with enough effort and momentum, it will spin itself around and around on its own. The hardest part is the beginning to get it spinning, and then it gets easier and easier to spin with each iteration.

This flywheel effect was popularized by business author Jim Collins in the book *Good to Great* on how to make successful businesses. His follow-up guidebook, *Turning the Flywheel*, takes the idea deeper. I'm just applying his excellent concept to real estate investing since you are buying a small real estate business with each property you own.

The flywheel for real estate investing consists of four parts, which I'm going to delve into in more detail as we move through this chapter. It's something to which I'll be referring as we go forward as well. Here are the four parts of the flywheel:

- Knowledge

- Confidence

- Action

- Experience

You start at the top of the wheel, at knowledge, and move around the flywheel until you arrive at the top again. Jim Collins chose a flywheel because, in addition to being round and therefore infinite, a flywheel is a fantastic engineering device that allows for the collection of and conservation of energy that can be used later on. And with each round trip around your flywheel, you're going to become stronger and increase the power of your investing career.

So let's take our first trip around your REI Flywheel.

Stage 1: Knowledge

It's said that knowledge is power. I believe this is true. Yet there's a little more to it than that. Knowledge is only power when you put it to use.

If, for example, our buddy Lenny the Landlord reads a book on making beer at home, he's learned some new knowledge. Yet until he actually creates his first brew, Landlord Lager, the knowledge doesn't really give him any power, does it? However, once Lenny puts his beer-making knowledge to use and creates his delicious brew, he now has the power to get inebriated or at least argue that his particular favorite football team is better than yours as loudly and incoherently as possible.

Well, real estate investing requires knowledge too—applied knowledge. This book is one form of knowledge, and there are lots of others. I mentioned earlier that unlike many forms of investing, real estate does come with a fairly steep learning curve, at least if you want to be successful at it.

However, unless and until you take the knowledge you've learned so far, including what you'll learn in this book, out into the real world and make something happen with it, well, you won't have empowered yourself. In other words, the flywheel doesn't get moving.

Do you know that I actually was going to go to college to learn real estate investing? Doesn't that sound crazy? Yet something stopped me—the idea that college is what you do if you're going to go and work for somebody else. Self-knowledge that you apply is what entrepreneurs do.

Rather than trying to get a degree in real estate theory, I decided that I could spend the same $100,000 I'd have given to the school in the form of tuition and use it to buy my first rental property. Yes, I read a bunch of books and asked a lot of questions. Yet it wasn't until I went out and did something that my real estate investing career took off. And that was when my personal flywheel began to spin.

After I read a few books, I had the confidence to start applying my knowledge. This book, and understanding the concepts in this book, is all the knowledge you will need to buy your first property. You may want to specialize in certain areas of real estate and want to gain more knowledge after your first purchase, and I will always encourage you to read as much as possible on the subject, or listen to real estate podcasts, or watch @TheHouseOfAC videos on YouTube.

And once you are done with this book or acquire all the knowledge you think you need to consume, you'll have the confidence to go buy a house in the next three months and guess what? Confidence is the second stage of the flywheel.

Stage 2: Confidence

This is an important stage in your investing development because it bolsters your actions. When you read the books, listen to the podcasts, and develop your knowledge base for the specific investing category you're interested in, you're ready to go out into the world.

Your knowledge-backed confidence gives you the comfort level to start talking to sellers, real estate agents, lenders, and more. You'll know what questions to ask them and how to analyze a deal. Additionally, you'll be more comfortable networking, which is a critical part of real estate investing. (Don't worry introverts, this can be done over email.)

A savvy and successful investor doesn't do it alone. The truth is that as you start acquiring properties, you're going to develop a team that helps you along the way. That's why connecting with other investors, lenders, agents, contractors, and other related professionals will expand your power to find and close the kinds of deals you're looking for. I will talk about building a team soon.

With the knowledge under your belt, you'll understand the process. You'll be able to speak the lingo and perform the proper calculations. You'll be able to talk intelligently about real estate investing with your friends and family and, more importantly, with other investors, industry professionals, and, of course, sellers.

Confidence takes your knowledge and keeps moving the flywheel forward to the next crucial step of any deal, and that is taking action. Action is the third part of our flywheel.

Stage 3: Action

Ahh, now it's time to put your money where your mouth is, where the rubber meets the road, where it's now time to expel post-digested food stuffs or remove yourself from the porcelain collection and disposal unit, if you know what I mean.

With the right knowledge and the confidence to use it, we now come to the action stage of your REI Flywheel. This is the applied knowledge part. So it's time for you to

- Network,
- Look at properties,
- Talk to sellers,

- Eek, make an offer,
- Put the property under contract, and
- Officially buy your first investment property.

I'll get into more detail on this process later on, yet this is where you actually go out into the world and put that knowledge and confidence to work. Until you do this, until you stop researching and talking about it and actually take real actions that lead to a deal, you're not a real estate investor and you are not on any track to FIRE.

However, once you get that flywheel turning, you'll cross an invisible barrier that 95% of all people who want to invest in real estate never cross. You're finally taking control of your future and becoming a bona fide real estate investor. It just takes one property to call yourself that. One property to drastically set you up to kill bills and change your financial future.

Stage 4: Experience

This is what you earn when you complete the first three sections of the flywheel. Experience only comes after acquiring knowledge, feeling confident, and going out there and taking action. It's in this stage where you've finally

- Bought a property,
- Bumbled through two dozen conversations with sellers,
- Stumbled through showings with tenants,
- Flew by the seat of your pants when negotiating with contractors,
- BS'd your way through a local Real Estate Investors Association meeting or ten, and
- Felt scared, excited, and relieved.

Don't worry, all of this is perfectly normal. Well, normal in the sense that all new investors go through these growing pains. The nice part is that there's no such thing as normal in real estate investing. Everybody handles all of the stages of investing differently. Different folks write leases different ways, qualify tenants in different ways, collect rent in different ways, and schedule fix-ups differently and so on.

The beauty of real estate is that it's not like learning an instrument. You don't have to play the piano with these specific fingers on this specific key in this specific way or you won't advance as a pianist. Or learning to shoot a basketball where you have to have the almost perfect shooting form to advance through the ranks. Landlording is very much the wild, wild West where any approach can work. Lenny makes up half the shit he does and he only gets richer from it.

The only person who's going to know that you may be winging it is you, so don't worry about it. Experience is the best teacher of all and makes all the books and videos pale in comparison. Think about the worst landlord you ever had—that's your bar. Just match or exceed that idiot.

Anybody can read about cage diving with sharks, but until you strap on a tank and try to tickle an eighteen-foot Great White on the belly with a starfish, you haven't really learned to cage dive now have you?

Real estate investing is exactly the same. Exactly, except for almost every aspect of the previous analogy. No sharks. No cages. With the experience you've gained from your first property, you've now come full circle and arrived back at the knowledge section of the flywheel.

You've now learned from your mistakes as well as your successes. Your experience has shown you things that you didn't even know you didn't know. Now you're ready for your next property, and with the experience from the first one, you can focus your next round of knowledge a bit more.

You don't have to read all the books again, of course. Now you can simply review the information that truly applied to your first property and that you now know will apply to your next. You might even have an idea of the kind of mentor you'd like to have as well.

You're ready to go around the flywheel again for your second property, then your third, fourth, and fifth. By the time you go around five times, you're going to be a truly savvy and experienced investor. You'll probably want to write your own book, and I'd be happy to write the foreword for you.

Believe it or not, I've gone through this process myself over 150 times personally in my investing career through the buying and selling and renting processes. Even more than that, I've actually gone through it with my real estate investing clients an additional 500 times. And you know what? I'm *still* learning. I still feel like an idiot more often than not, and I've accepted it. Real estate is an ever-changing game.

Each trip around the REI Flywheel I learn something new, and, honestly, it's really fun. So now that you understand the process, let's go forward and talk some more specifics and see what interesting experiences or tortures we can subject our buddy Lenny the Landlord to.

5

"Alan, are you sure P-ing on a FIRE is really what you want me to focus on?"

Umm, it feels like you just overhead someone's conversation about this book in a crowded restaurant or you have confused me with a different potty-mouthed author. I want to make it clear I don't suggest urinating on fires for TikTok views as a path to FIRE. This zany action may work for some aspiring entrepreneur with bladder control issues, but I'm entirely on a different P that makes you money. Specifically the 4 Ps.

This is where we start talking dollars and cents and where you see all the ways that you can make money in real estate to help you avoid pissing out your FIRE, which is, of course, your plan to be financially independent and retire early.

Not every type of investment will yield all four of these profit centers, or Ps, yet if you can get three out of four at least, then you're in good shape.

Why can't you get all four all the time?

Well, that'll make more sense after we go through the Ps, yet the simple answer is that not every property provides cash flow. Rentals do, but flips don't. A marina does but a piece of vacant land doesn't, or usually doesn't.

There's an old saying that states that money is made in real estate when you *buy* and not when you *sell*. That saying primarily refers to rental property and isn't entirely accurate. You certainly can make money when you sell, yet what the phrase means is that on the day you close, your property analysis numbers should show you a profit, whether that's rental income or the after-rehab value of a flip.

So let's dive deeper into the 4 Ps, and I'll explain how each one works and how you can profit from it. I honestly hope you are here for the profit talk and not the potty talk.

Profit Area #1: Appreciation

You're probably already familiar with this one. Most people are. You buy a house for $100K and then sell it in fifteen years for $150K. The property has appreciated in value $50K for a variety of reasons:

- Market goes up
- Surrounding areas are developed
- Improved shopping and schools in the area
- A growing job market

With single family dwellings like houses, condos, and even multifamily properties up to four units, the appreciation usually happens based on one or more of the reasons I just listed. Of course, as we all know, property values can fall as well. However, if you take the average over the past 100 years or so, real estate does go up at about 1.5 to 2% per year after adjusting for inflation, even if there is a temporary downturn.

Now don't ever expect this type of appreciation as a reason to buy a home, because you can't really control a lot of this. I consider each home I buy to come with an imaginary lottery ticket of potential big appreciation outside of my control: let's say the city turns the adjacent landfill into a new park, or the abandoned railroad station around the corner turns into a hipster food hall, or the neighborhood just launched an amazing new charter school that teaches your kids six languages and guarantees entrance into an Ivy League school. These events will greatly affect your appreciation, or equity in your home, without you having to do anything. You are making money for nothing, just like with a lottery ticket.

On the other hand, larger multifamily properties like apartments, marinas, and mobile home parks appreciate a little differently. You can increase the perceived value of the property, or equity, through improvements and the addition of amenities and by increasing rents and reducing expenses. This is also true for commercial properties and industrial parks as well.

Naturally, you can inflate the value of a single family home the same way. For instance, you could buy a fixer-upper and do some cosmetic repairs that both increase the resale value as well as the potential rental price. This is appreciation via sweat equity and something you do have control over. Yet for the most part, passive appreciation and the increasing of your home's equity happens slowly over time.

Profit Area #2: Positive Cash Flow

This is pretty much everybody's favorite, including mine. It's how I will HELLFIRE. There's nothing better than purchasing an investment that begins to pay you back immediately, is there? And unlike most asset classes, rental real estate does this on a regular basis and in some particularly cool ways. What's really exciting is that there are actually many kinds of income-generating property, for example:

- Single family houses, trailers, or condos
- Mobile home parks with lot, or land, rents
- Apartment complexes or buildings
- Marinas
- Office buildings or parks
- Industrial parks
- Self-storage
- Parking lots
- Leasing land to businesses—called triple net leases

Cash flow of course comes when you purchase a property and offer it for rent, just as Lenny the Landlord did in chapter 2. He purchased four single family homes and rented them out. After he set aside money for maintenance, management, and other expenses and after he paid the mortgage, Lenny had a source of passive positive cash flow.

Here's what's really cool about cash flow. Just as the property appreciates over time, so, too, can your stream of income from a particular property. Annual rent raises continually increase your ROI. This can be done as a matter of course or after some improvement. There is one aspect of cash flow that every investor should understand: net operating income or NOI.

NOI is what's left from your gross income after subtracting expenses. These expenses might include maintenance, vacancy, management, and utilities or services. They *do not* include debt service, which is your mortgage payment. That's an important distinction that you should keep in mind.

NOI = Gross income – expenses

Once you have the NOI of an income-generating property, that's what you use to pay your mortgage, and whatever is left is your positive (hopefully) cash flow. And this cash flow is what I want you to use to cover your life expenses to House FIRE like me. But there is more money to be made and more Ps in this real estate pod, so keep reading.

Profit Area #3: Principal Paydown

With P3, you have another area where you make money in real estate: equity via principal paydown. Equity is the difference between what a property is worth or sells for and what you owe on it. Appreciation does build equity, of course, but in this section, I'm going to focus on the other direction.

You can think of equity being built forward and backward. Forward in the sense that your equity grows as your property appreciates as in P1. This is great, but you can't always control it.

On the other hand, you build equity backward by paying down the principal on any loans you have on the property. Let's use our old pal Lenny to illustrate:

Lenny purchases a $150,000 house and puts $30,000 down and gets a mortgage for $120,000. At the time of closing, Lenny's equity is $30K: $150K - $120K = $30K.

Lenny immediately built in $30K of equity with his down payment. Okay, great. Now, let's skip ahead five years. Lenny's property has appreciated by $30,000 up to $180,000, and he's been faithfully making his loan payments. Now, the truth is that most mortgages don't let you pay off the loan equally over the life of the loan. The fact is that most thirty-year loans are structured so that the first seven years of the loan are almost entirely interest. This lets the bank recoup their money in that time.

Amortization Schedule

Date	Interest	Principal	Balance
Month 1 of Year 1	$500	$144	$119,856
Month 2 of Year 1	$499	$145	$119,711
Month 3 of Year 1	$499	$145	$119,566
Month 4 of Year 1	$498	$146	$119,420
Month 5 of Year 1	$498	$147	$119,273
Month 6 of Year 1	$497	$147	$119,126
Month 7 of Year 1	$496	$148	$118,978
Month 8 of Year 1	$496	$148	$118,830
Month 9 of Year 1	$495	$149	$118,681
Month 10 of Year 1	$495	$150	$118,531
Month 11 of Year 1	$494	$150	$118,381
Month 12 of Year 1	$493	$151	$118,230
First Year of Payments	$5,960	$1,770	$118,230

However, if you average it out over thirty years, then each year you're buying down the initial loan amount by about 3% or a little higher. So let's figure that in Lenny's case, after five years, he's paid off 15% of his loan balance, or about $18,000 through principal paydown. Let's see where Lenny stands now: $180K new property value - $102,000 remaining balance on loan = $78,000 in equity.

So if Lenny were to sell the house right now, he'd pull out $78K in profit—well, minus closing costs, real estate commissions, and so on. Yet this is just a simple example to illustrate the power of principal paydown. Just making the minimum payments each month on your mortgage, your tenants are paying a portion of the loan principal and the loan interest. The principal portion being paid each month goes back to you in the form of increased home equity each month.

Some smug investors—by this I mean Lenny, who thinks he is smart and hip to this way of making money— will actually pump all his positive cash flow back into debt payoff so that he can both build more equity and pay off his loan sooner. But this is where good ol' Alan Corey comes in and smacks some sense into Lenny. I channel my inner Suge Knight and shake Lenny off a balcony by his ankles and tell him to stop, collaborate, and listen to this important advice:

Paying a little extra on your mortgage payment is dumb. (Dave Ramsey fans get ready to clutch your pearls.)

Let me explain. Remember when you were a kid and you'd walk into any diner with a jukebox and plop five pennies down on a counter to buy an ice cream cone? Well, I don't remember those days either. How old do you think I am? But I know you could, at one time, because when I walk into an antique shop, I see old metal signs advertising ice cream cones for a nickel. Nowhere in the world can you buy ice cream for this crazy price anymore and there is a reason why. This rising cost of all things is called inflation, and you should use it to your advantage.

A good way to look at inflation is to pretend you run your own business. Let's say you run the ice cream empire of Lennyville, and you sell all your ice cream cones for a nickel because that's what your rusted metal signs say you should sell them for. But then there is a drought, so that increases the cost of sugar, and you pass on that increase to your customers. So now you have to charge 10 cents a cone.

Then your cows get moody and won't produce high-quality milk unless they have weekly sessions with a lactation consultant, and this is an extra expense, which means you now have to charge 15 cents a cone to maintain profit margins. Well, eventually you have competitors from the next town over because your ice cream monopoly is obviously a cash cow, pun intended.

These new dairy farm competitors headhunt your best-of-the-best milkmaids by offering to pay them more money than you do, so you match their new offers so they don't leave. But in order to cover this increase in costs, you now charge 25 cents a cone. This goes on and on and eventually ice cream cones cost $5, jukeboxes disappear, and *milkmaids* is an offensive term.

So what does this have to do with paying a little extra on your mortgage payments? Well, let's say you have $1 in your pocket just begging to be spent. A gas-guzzling ice cream truck with a terrible jingle pulls up next to you, and it's advertising a special of $1 for a cone. Your dollar bill is exactly equal to one ice cream.

Likewise, your paper George Washington can be spent instead toward debt payoff because its purchasing power can reduce your mortgage principal by exactly $1. A formula for you mathletes: $1.00 in your pocket = 1 ice cream cone = $1.00 in mortgage principal paydown. Where to spend the dollar?

Lenny, although he is hanging upside down fifteen stories up and melting in the sun like a vanilla ice cream cone, still thinks being Lean FIRE-minded is smart. He is a cut-expenses-at-all-costs superhero.

He screams, "I will not buy the ice cream today, I'll pay an extra dollar on my mortgage payment and then in twenty years I'll buy ice cream every day when I have no mortgage payment."

But a House FIRE, live-above-your-means, savvy financial investor superhero shaking Lenny by his boots will shout, "No, let's buy ice cream! The mortgage can wait."

And this is the right move as my oversized belly confirms because I make this decision often. I know in thirty years a solar-powered ice cream Tesla Cybertruck will pull up next to me and say, "I've got an ice cream cone special of one cone for $3."

I have no money on me in this future cashless society, but I look around and find a discarded Sacagawea coin on the ground. It's basically worthless, as it will only buy 33% of an ice cream cone. However, it will still buy me $1 in mortgage principal paydown. In this future world, the one-dollar coin found on the ground = 1/3 of an ice cream cone = $1 in mortgage principal paydown.

My coin has less purchasing power but still pays the same amount off my debt. So why not wait to pay off my $1 in debt when my $1 is only worth 33 cents in the future?

And this inflation principle is why you want money today and why the following statements are true:

- The US national debt will never be paid off. It's advantageous to pay your loans down in the future when money is worth less.

- The mortgage payment you pay is mostly interest at the start of your loan and then mostly principal at the end of the loan. The banks want their money sooner rather than later to account for inflation.

- A long-term fixed-rate loan will feel like it is getting cheaper over time. Technically you are making the same payment each month, but if you have a mortgage that is a fixed rate at 4% over thirty years and inflation increases at an average of 2% a year, you are paying off your loan with cheaper dollars the longer you have the loan. It doesn't matter what portion of the loan payment is interest or principal, a dollar tomorrow is cheaper than a dollar today.

- 1990s rapper Vanilla Ice was rumored to gift the rights to his one-hit wonder "Ice Ice Baby" to Suge Knight's gang after being threatened to be dropped off his high-rise balcony.

Sorry, that was a weird tangent, but it got you to Google that crazy Vanilla Ice story didn't it? But let's get back to principal paydown—it's a great thing. Just let your tenants pay it down for you. Even if Lenny was renting out this property and was just breaking even over the past five years for $0 in cash flow each month, he is still making money on the property with the tenants paying down this mortgage balance for him. But Lenny himself does not need to make additional principal payments to benefit from using Profit Area #3.

Profit Area #4: Preferential Tax Benefits

Would you believe that good old Uncle Sam actually *wants* to give real estate investors a break? That it's indeed true that the US government is secretly designed to make the rich richer?

Well, okay, that second part isn't true because there isn't anything secret about it. The IRS does in fact give tax advantages to promote investing. I touched on this briefly in chapter 2 when comparing Lenny's buying an all-cash property vs. leveraging four rentals. If you recall, as landlords, we get to take two distinct write-offs, and the first of these actually features two separate types as well.

Let me explain, because, if you are like me, taxes make my head spin.

You probably already know about the mortgage interest deduction. Pretty much anybody can take this one on their taxes by itemizing their deductions. It allows you to deduct any interest paid on a home loan as a tax write-off, thus decreasing your taxable income and lowering your adjusted gross. This is especially good news for investors—investors who use leverage, that is.

The second category of tax deductions is depreciation. Depreciation is literally an accounting entry where real property can be divided by a certain figure and then that number is written off as decreased value or a phantom loss on paper. With real estate, depreciation is a huge tax ally to the investor.

- **Building depreciation** is where the value of the structure is calculated and then divided by 27.5 years. This number is your annual deduction.

Let's take a look at an example of how depreciation works with our newly enlightened friend Lenny the Landlord. We'll assume that Lenny has purchased a $200,000 home with $50K down and a $150K mortgage. He rents the place out for $1,850 per month. Here's a quick snapshot of what this looks like on an annual basis:

- Annual Gross Income: $22,200
- Annual Mortgage Payment: $9,660 ($805 a month)
- Annual Expenses (insurance, maintenance, property taxes, etc.): $6,200 ($517 a month)
- Annual Positive Cash Flow: $6,340

Pretty good return, right? Well, Lenny still has to pay taxes on the $16,000 he earned after subtracting expenses. Assuming a 30% tax bracket, that means he owes close to $4,800 in taxes a year. A good calculation to run is cash-on-cash return. This calculates how much cash Lenny puts in a deal and his return on only that cash he invested. Lenny invested $50,000 and makes $6,340 a year. After tax, he profits $1,540 a year. The cash-on-cash formula of NOI/total cash invested shows us that, after taxes, Lenny is getting a 3% cash-on-cash return from this property.

That's not the best return for $50,000 spent, right?

Well, that's not quite how it works because Lenny is going to take the tax deductions I talked about. First, 75% of Lenny's mortgage payment goes to interest payments to be used in mortgage interest deductions. Second, land doesn't depreciate, only houses do. So let's assume the land is worth 20% of the $200,000 purchase price, or $40,000. That means the house value is $160,000.

Mortgage interest deduction: $9,660 x 75% = $7,245
Building depreciation:
$160K building value ($200K - $40K)
$160K/27.5 = $5,818

Things are starting to look different, aren't they? Let's take a look at the income numbers again with all these deductions:

- Gross Income: $22,200

- Expenses: $6,200

- Mortgage Interest Deduction: $7,245

- Building Depreciation: $5,818

When you subtract all the deductions and expenses, you end up with a new and a lower taxable income figure of $2,737. With this accounting, Lenny is only paying taxes on 43% of his annual cash flow of $6,340.

See how the rich get richer? Or to put it another way, he's just increased his cash-on-cash return from this house by 4.2% and brought it up to 7.2% because of tax breaks. Isn't that awesome? If this tax talk is making your eyelids heavy, this is what you get a CPA for; they are worth the price in the money they can save you.

See why I say rental real estate is the best of all?

In the next chapter, I'm going to take things a step further and talk about focusing your efforts on a specific strategy within real estate investing. Maybe being a landlord and holding a property for ten years or more doesn't get your blood pumping. Maybe you want to flip homes and earn huge windfalls in exchange for higher risk like they do on all those TV shows.

Sure, house flips don't have the great tax breaks of long-term buy and holds I just explained, but you could do four flips a year where the profit from the fourth flip covers the entire tax bill of all four. You are just using a flip to kill the bill this way instead of with rental cash flow. This is perfectly acceptable too. Of course, flipping really lets you accelerate your journey around the REI Flywheel and grow strong as an investor since speed in acquiring homes and renovating them quickly is the name of the game. Let's examine this aspect of House FIRE a little more.

6

"Wait, Alan, in a heated market do you want me to flip homes or rent them out?"

Well, questioning reader, it's your choice. One of my favorite things about real estate investing is the huge number of options it gives you to achieve your House FIRE dreams. You can choose from a million ways to make a million dollars in real estate.

You can FIRE (the concept of being financially independent and retiring early) by using any of these strategies as a real estate investor:

- You can be the off-market deal hound.
- You can be the small deal finder.
- You could get into new construction.

- You can be a real estate agent for extra savings or extra income.
- You could become a condo queen/king and be an expert in a niche.
- You could be the multifamily magnate of your city.
- You might be a row house renovator.
- You might be a hard-money lender for other investors.
- You may be a remote out-of-state investor who invests only in lower cost of living communities.
- You could be the wholesaler extraordinaire to make deals happen with no up-front money.
- You can be an identical twin and cohost a dozen different property-themed TV shows.

That's just the tip of the iceberg. Opportunity abounds in real estate whether you're just getting started and only have a few thousand to invest all the way up to putting millions into huge skyscrapers.

Flipping homes can allow you to generate more income quickly so you can apply them to a larger portfolio of buy-and-hold rentals later. And house flipping zips you through five cycles of the REI Flywheel superfast. There is an advantage to each strategy, and you as an investor probably have a natural inclination to which approach works best for you. It's important to know about all the strategies, but not necessarily to act on each of them, in order to successfully House FIRE.

It's vital that you understand that, when getting into real estate investing, you want to be very specific. The more focused you are, the easier it is to hit your target. And that starts with the type of investing you want to do. So in this chapter, I'm showing you four common strategies to choose from, and I encourage you to pick one strategy and own it. Jumping from strategy to strategy is like jumping from flywheel to flywheel and, thus, is not a good use of momentum, or more specifically: knowledge, confidence, action, and experience.

These are the four easiest strategies that lend themselves well to success for your first five deals:

- Buy and hold
- Fix and flip
- Fix and hold
- Hold and fix

I'm going to go through each one in more detail.

Strategy #1: Buy and Hold

This is probably the easiest of the strategies. It's the get-rich-slow track, yet it's the most natural place to make your first jump. Generally, it takes less money to get into this type of investing and less time. I prefer this strategy for long-term bill killing and the other strategies for extra income options. You buy a renovated property that needs little to no work and you rent it out. It's the basic investor approach.

Buy and holds have the tax advantages I mentioned earlier, which makes for a smart long-term approach. You don't really need any special skills to purchase and manage buy and holds, and these properties tend to give you cash flow right from day one. It's also fairly easy to get a mortgage to purchase this kind of investment. And it's really easy to pass off this investment to a property manager if you'd like.

On the other hand, it's hard if not impossible to increase the value of this type of property through sweat equity if you are buying an already renovated buy and hold. In this strategy, you're not going in with the idea of making big improvements. The only work you do here is to keep the property in the same basic condition you bought it in. This attracts good renters and keeps your cash flowing regularly. Basically, this strategy gets you into a turnkey rental property. This is one that Lenny really enjoys, because as soon as he gets a tenant into it, he can start collecting profits. Here's how that works:

Lenny finds a three-bedroom, two-bath home of about 1,400 square feet in a decent neighborhood. The seller is asking $150,000, and Lenny knows through his market research that he can rent it for $1,500 per month.

With $30,000 down and a $120K mortgage at 5% interest rate, his mortgage payment with taxes and property insurance (known as PITI, principal, interest, tax, and insurance) will be around $900 a month. Lenny adds in maintenance costs of $100 a month to a future repair budget. His annual expenses total out at $12,000 a year on this property.

For income, Lenny also budgets for a month of vacancy between tenants moving in and moving out so his annual rental income pencils out at $16,500 in annual rent ($1,500 x 11 months). Lenny knows if everything goes to plan, he'll make $4,500 a year, and he can pay himself back his $30,000 at the end of five years. If Lenny is buying one property a year over five years, by the time Lenny looks to buy his sixth property, he will be getting his full payment back on his first property:

- Purchase price: $150,000
- Down payment: $30,000
- Rental amount: $1,500 a month/$18,000 a year
- Mortgage: $900 a month/$10,800 a year
- Expense budget: $100 a month/$1,200 a year
- Vacancy budget: $125 a month/$1,500 (one month's rent)
- Cash flow = $375 a month/$4,500 year

At the end of five years, Lenny has gotten about $2,200 in principal paydown and $27,000 in cash flow for a total of $29,200, which matches up closely to the $30,000 he invested to buy the house. This is, of course, without raising rents and staying within his maintenance budget.

We think it should be fine since he bought a renovated house to begin with and major repairs already completed. This math is also assuming the tenant moves out every year and Lenny takes a month to refill it. In Lenny's eyes, it's a free home to Lenny moving forward at this point, and infinite return time again.

Listen, I know you might not get the exact same numbers as Lenny. Maybe in your market your cash flow is going to be lower, or the purchase price is going to be higher, or interest rates are different depending when you are reading this amazing book for the twentieth time. The important point is the math and how to look at a deal. If this isn't for you, I have three more strategies to tackle.

Strategy #2: Fix and Flip

This is probably the strategy most folks are familiar with. Flipping houses is popular in an up-trending market, which we've had for over a decade now. How many reality TV shows do you know that focus on buying, fixing, and selling properties? It's basically the entire programming of HGTV for a reason: it's fun and exciting and makes for good stories of creating your own gold mine. And only on TV can someone scream at contractors over and over and they don't ever walk off the site.

It's in this strategy that large short-term gains are made. However, money made from flipping is heavily taxed. Also, it takes a considerable amount of money to invest before you see large returns. You have to purchase the property, hold it, fix it, and sell it. This strategy requires capital and speed to be successful.

Because moving quickly is a key ingredient, this strategy does let you spin around the REI Flywheel the fastest, as you might expect. Opportunities in this strategy range from simple cosmetic repairs to major renovations and additions even to complete teardown and rebuilds. Let's take a look at a simple example that Lenny is considering:

While I'm not going to get into a lot of details here, because fix and flip is a big topic that requires its own knowledge base, I'll just give you a taste. There are four basic costs that have to be calculated when considering doing a fix-up. Additionally, you have to get pretty good at determining the final sale price, or what flippers call the after-rehab value (ARV).

In order to do that, you have to consider these costs:

- Purchase price
- Cost of repairs
- Holding costs
- Minimum profit

The first two are obvious. How much do you buy the house for and how much will it cost to fix it up? The third item, holding costs, is represented by the cost of utilities, insurance, property taxes, and mortgage payments while you own the property as it is being fixed up. Minimum profit is up to you to see if all the work, effort, and risk are worth the reward, or profit, at the end.

So Lenny finds a 3/2 that needs some cosmetic updates and a few major repairs. His estimates are all based on a ninety-day turnaround:

- Purchase price: $100,000
- Estimated repairs: $40,000
- Holding costs: $5,000

Now I'm keeping this simple. I haven't included closing costs on buying a home, but let's say we got the seller to cover the closing costs. All savvy flippers also include a minimum profit in each calculation—the lowest amount of money they'll need to earn to make the deal worthwhile. Let's say that Lenny wants at least $15,000 in profit.

When you add all of these numbers, you get a total cost for this deal of $160,000. So that means that this is the absolute lowest price that Lenny can accept for this flip after he fixes it up in order to make his $15,000 minimum profit.

Well, let's say Lenny doesn't have his head in his ass and that he did a good job of analyzing the deal and the market and ran a strong comparative sales analysis on similar homes in the area to determine the right way to flip this property. That, plus a good quality renovation that had buyers swooning, led to a bidding war on the home when he put it on the market. He accepts an offer for $180,000—making a profit of $25,000.

Pretty good, right? Well, depending on several factors, Lenny is going to have to pay anywhere from $6,000 to $8,000 in short-term capital gains taxes. That kind of stinks, yet if Lenny could repeat this process *every* ninety days, he's still created an after-tax income of $68,000 per year, right? And he zipped through the REI Flywheel four times and gained a ton of experience, confidence, and knowledge along the way.

In terms of House FIRE with this strategy, you are creating short windfalls for yourself and it's anything but passive. When Lenny wants to retire early, he'll want to reinvest some of those profits into strategy #1 with buy-and-hold rentals, or, better yet, he's primed himself really well to do the next strategy.

Strategy #3: Fix and Hold

This strategy combines the best of the first two. Here, you find a distressed property that needs some work, buy it cheap, and then fix it up. Rather than sell it, though, you then put it on the rental market and start earning cash flow. This way, your capital is protected as equity in the property and you get to benefit from the two big tax breaks I talked about in the last chapter: building depreciation and mortgage interest deduction.

It's this strategy where larger returns on both your capital and your cash flow can be found. You can take this strategy further by using the BRRRR method, or Buy, Rehab, Rent, Refinance, and Repeat. This strategy is promoted in a book by uber-popular real estate investor and *BiggerPockets* podcaster Brandon Turner. I touched on this at the beginning of the book as a way to create infinite returns, but let me explain by using old Lenny again to drive the point home.

Lenny looks at the house from the last section and figures that instead of selling, he's gonna buy it, fix it, and rent it. Most of the same stuff applies, with the exception of the minimum profit margin. He figures that he can get the place for $75K and rent it as is, but he'd rather put $45K into it and then rent it out for more money and not worry about doing major repairs later.

So Lenny buys his $75,000 house for 25% down payment, or $18,750. Let's round up to $20,000. Plus he has earmarked $45,000 for a renovation budget. Let's call it $50,000 for loan expenses, carrying costs, and utility bills while doing the renovation. Okay, Lenny is in for $70,000 total on this house.

Lenny figures the house will be worth $180K after being rehabbed. After he completes his home makeover, this newly renovated house will rent for $1,500 per month in this neighborhood.

- $75,000 purchase price
- $50,000 renovation budget
- Lenny's out-of-pocket $70,000 (down payment and rehab budget)
- Mortgage of $56,250 at 5.5% = $325 a month
- Lenny rents it out for $1,475

After calculating a one-month vacancy and $100 a month repair budget, Lenny is looking at a cash flow of $725 a month.

Monthly Expenses

Mortgage = $325

Insurance = $100

Taxes = $150

Repairs = $100

Vacancy = $75

Total = $750

Monthly Rent: $1,475

Monthly Cash Flow = $1,475 - $750 = $725

Even ignoring the great tax breaks in this calculation, Lenny's got a pretty good seat at the FIRE pit, right? If this was 1999, Lenny could chill with Destiny's Child with a promise to cover their "telephone bills, their automo bills" and eventually more bills.

Well, now comes the refinance aspect of BRRRR: After about a year of getting a decent return on his money, Lenny decides it's time to pull his home equity out with a cash-out refinance. He has a $55K mortgage or so on the house after a year of principal paydown, and he wants to pull out his initial $70K.

Lenny's timing is atrocious though. The market has dipped, and after the bank sends an appraiser over, the value comes back at $170,000, $10,000 shy of what Lenny had anticipated. Interest rates have shot up recently and lending has tightened, and the bank will only loan him 75% of the appraised value, or $127,500, instead of his expected 80% appraised value. Regardless, Lenny still moves forward with the cash-out refinance.

With these numbers, Lenny still pays off the previous mortgage of $55,000 and gets the difference back to him in a check of $72,500.

- $170,000 appraised value
- New mortgage $127,500
- Pay off old mortgage of $55,000
- Check to Lenny for difference = $72,500
- New mortgage amount $850 a month
- New cash flow to Lenny = $200 a month

He's got his $70K back, and that $70K is tax-free, and he can do it all over again (the repeat part of BRRRR). He's gone around the REI Flywheel and can get going on his next purchase. He keeps a buy-and-hold rental for himself with cash flow and kills some bills with it. He's in infinite return territory. Lenny will recycle his money over and over to build a small rental portfolio using the same down payment and rehab cash again and again.

But why do a cash-out refinance when the market has dropped? Why not just keep the extra cash flow to kill more bills? Well, Lenny wants more cash to buy cheaper homes of course. He also wants to take all his money out of the property to make it risk-free. If something happens and he has to foreclose on it, worst case scenario, he only hurts his pride and dings his credit score. That's how an investor thinks. No money is actually lost in the process of this worst case scenario since he has it in his pocket or, more likely, reinvesting in another BRRRR. If Lenny invested in the stock market and had the same loss, the money may be long gone with little hope for it to return.

It won't take Lenny long to be roasting marshmallows at his FIRE pit, if he just did this strategy. Endless retirement s'mores anyone? No? Okay, so if this strategy is not for you either, then I've got one more.

Strategy #4: Hold and Fix

In this scenario, you buy a place that is dated and aged and simply do Band-Aid fix-ups to keep it at about the same level as it was when you acquired it. You do just enough to keep things running, but don't invest heavily in upgrades. You save the renovation budget until later, maybe right before you sell it or refinance it or when a renovation is cheaper than the fix itself.

Part of the reason for this is that you may have a property in an area that doesn't support the investment. Maybe when you buy the house, it'll get $950 per month, but it needs a new kitchen or floors or whatever. However, you determine that even if you put $10,000 into the place, it still won't rent for any more than $950. But maybe you like the long-term prospects of the neighborhood or you got a really good deal on a livable, but not sexy, home because it sat on the market a long time.

And another great reason to do this, you are waiting for other investors or homeowners to make the first move. You watch someone else renovate their home down the street first and try to rent it or sell it and see how successful they are. You are simply waiting and watching what others are able to do since time is not of the essence.

The goal here is to keep your home stable and watch the market. If the neighborhood suddenly starts rising in value, then you can do some rehab and sell the property for a profit and move on. Or renovate and charge higher rent down the line if the market tells you this area can support the higher rents because a neighbor just did it successfully.

There is money to be made here; you just have to be careful and make sure that the deal fits the following criteria:

- You can afford to do minimal wear and tear repairs and still maintain your profit margin.

- The purchase price allows this and reflects the situation. Home should feel like a bargain when you buy since it's not in pristine condition at time of purchase.

- The market supports the rent you need to charge in the current as-is condition of the home.

In this case, Lenny knows what rent he can collect in the home's current as-is condition as there is maybe a tenant already in place in the home or a similar home in the neighborhood has a tenant paying a price he knows he can get too. As long as it is cash-flow positive on day one and he sees possible future improvements in this neighborhood, he can save a portion of his cash and renovate it down the line.

Lenny just wants to buy the properties in this area for cheap now and cash in on the neighborhood improving later. It's a way to get on the property ladder without having a huge pile of money or a huge chunk of time to renovate a house immediately. It's a buy and hold like strategy #1, but with future upside possibilities as you can improve the property for extra equity when the time is right.

It's always good to have as many exit strategies as possible with any property you buy, and this strategy gives you the most exits. It doesn't matter if he sells in one year or ten years, he can count on any of these exit strategies:

1. Sell the house with no money spent on renovations in same condition he bought it in. If he sells for the same price he bought it, Lenny still made some cash flow rental income and had principal paydown and some tax breaks during his hold period.

2. Make small cosmetic updates to the house to get a higher paying tenant with the home's current floor plan. Maybe do a small project every couple of years each time a tenant moves out—a bathroom one year, a kitchen the next.

3. Make major renovations to the house—spend on additions, adding a second story, remove walls to change to an open floor plan. Once Lenny's able to save up for a large renovation budget or to qualify for a big renovation loan from a mortgage lender, he can go big. Maybe Lenny recognizes a huge financial gain in having more square footage added. He can still keep it either as a rental (pivot to strategy #1) or sell it if he wants (pivot to strategy #2).

4. Launch a minor or a major renovation to the house and use the BRRRR method to do a cash-out refinance and keep it as a rental (pivot to strategy #3).

5. Put no money in renovations and sell to a builder to tear it down and build new construction if the house is on its last legs or if the neighborhood is supporting new construction builds and prices.

6. Put big money into it and tear down and build new construction himself.

7. Provide all tenants with unlimited Viagra, free Netflix and chill subscriptions, and a heart-shaped

Jacuzzi until a famous person is born in the house so you can turn it into a museum later.

Wow, that's seven exit strategies for Lenny and three different ways to pivot to each of the other strategies and one surefire way to be labeled a creeper. These multiple outs is how you "get lucky" in real estate. You have as many properties as possible and figure out how best to pivot or exit each home based on what the market is telling you at that moment in time.

No matter which of the four strategies you choose, you or Lenny can make money and be successful. They all fall into the REI Flywheel. The point, though, is to pick one and stick to it through your first five properties if possible. After that, if you want to branch out, go for it. Yet for your first five, it's vital you stick to your guns and really master one strategy if you can or master one pivot if you go with strategy #4.

Once you pick a strategy you are going to focus on, then it's time to choose a product. By that I mean a highly specific type of property in which to invest. I'm going to explore that further in the next chapter, but circle one of these first before moving on to the next chapter.

Investing Strategy
Buy + Hold
Fix + Flip
Fix + Hold
Hold + Fix

7

"Alan, WTH are product types in real estate? Explain it like I'm five years old and playing with matches, please."

No problem, kiddo. Now that you've chosen an investment strategy, we need to put that strategy to work on acquiring a specific type of product. By product I mean property type. So far, we've already seen that our good buddy Lenny the Landlord likes the buy-and-hold strategy, and he's chosen single family homes—or at least he has until we manipulate him into doing our bidding. Muahahahaha!

However, like any good map, this one should not simply contain directions. I want to provide you with some guidance on what pitfalls to avoid. Pitfalls that could slow you down or even lead to a major derailment. It's great to know the path you're taking, but it also takes a sharp eye to know when you come across a nice cow pie so you don't step in it, am I right?

So let us begin with what *not* to invest in on your first few properties. And, no, this isn't some reverse psychology where the evil Doctor Corey insidiously leads you into his trap. Over my years of investing, I've discovered a few traps to watch out for. Some through trial and error, some through mentors of my own, and some by observing my clients. Please take special note of this next section.

What Not to Invest In

You are at risk of falling into some easy traps when it comes to real estate investing, especially for the new and excited investor. One of the most common traps to avoid is this one: **Don't invest in something you want to live in yourself.**

Please keep in mind that you're not buying your personal residence. You're not buying a property that you'd like to move into. You're buying a small business, and the best small businesses are the ones that utilize the best balance of price and quality, risk and reward.

Sure we all want to personally live in the best school districts, near the hippest goatee and flannel coffee shops, near the cool music venue, across from the most beautiful park in town, or Lenny's rental home where Ryan Gosling was conceived. Naturally. Yet these properties are the ones that command a premium to buy and may not support your investment strategy.

Go and buy your next primary residence there—but not a rental. These areas have already been gentrified and improved. They're already expensive and are most likely to level off. A savvy investor wants to buy something a little further down the food chain—a property in a neighborhood that's still up and coming. An area that already has renters. You can search Zillow for past and present neighborhood rental listings and get an idea of how many homes are for rent and what the rental prices are on average. An area that, through your own efforts, may increase in desirability and, by extension, boost the value of your investment, be it in equity or in potential rental income.

Think of it like this: Real estate investing is a spreadsheet decision, not an "I'd like to live here" decision. You're not looking for the Instagram-worthy house with granite, hardwood, and marble. You're looking for a solid property that most people want to rent or buy. Most renters aren't willing to pay extra for these niceties, even if they want them. Most buyers of a flip want something upgraded, but if you take it too far in a neighborhood that won't support it, you're simply putting too much money into a project.

Remember, each property is a small business and a small business is evaluated on how much money it makes, not on how expensive the countertops are. Let people judge you on your bank account, not on where you invest.

A rental isn't a showpiece. What tenants want most isn't flash. They want security and predictability. They want to get their money's worth and find something decent in their price range. Remember my friend with the vaulted ceiling upgrades? Buying in already established areas is this on steroids.

I'm not saying you will lose money buying in these areas, just that you likely will make more money if you invested elsewhere. Buying in primo nabes is like buying bonds—a very safe investment with very low returns. Not the end of the world, but it'll be a slower path to House FIRE where you become financially independent and retire early.

I know, a brand new shiny house that you buy or that you even build might seem like a great idea. Everything is in top quality and you can get top dollar. Yet therein lies the problem: **Avoid new construction.**

You see, my dear reader, the best investments are those that are underpriced, underappreciated, and under duress. If you get a brand new home, all that's going to happen is that it's slowly going to decrease in value, at least in terms of the wear and tear. Not to mention it's going to be sold at top dollar when you buy. You don't want to get into a hold-and-fix situation with a new home. Better to find something older that you can get at a discount if this is your strategy.

Think of it like this: What's the better financial decision? Buying a brand new car at retail—say $35K—or buying one that's a year or two old at half the price? The lady who drives off in the brand new car has to pay all that interest on something that immediately loses value when she drives off the lot. On the other hand, the lady who buys one that's *nearly* new for $20K is getting a car that's worth what she's paying and she won't take the big depreciation hit.

Both cars get her to my book signing at the exact same speed, and that's the most important thing to think about when buying any car. She might as well save $15K and use the money instead on a rental home purchase.

You do save on capital expenditures with buying new construction. You probably won't have to buy a new roof, HVAC, or water heater anytime soon. But you really limit your exit strategies with this property. You can either (a) rent as is or (b) sell as is. The new construction builder took value-add benefits off the table.

Now consider this: Land! Land! They ain't makin' it anymore, ya know. That's true, however, buying vacant land isn't an investment, it's speculation. **Avoid vacant land.**

The difference is simple: An investment makes you money immediately or at least in the short term, while a speculation takes a long time to pay off and may or may not pay off down the road. In the time you're waiting for the payoff, you still owe property tax on the land, so it's not an asset that pays for itself but a liability that takes money out of your pocket.

Sure, a lucky land speculator might buy $100K worth of vacant land and in five years sell it for $500K when the town expands and somebody wants that land for a shopping center or neighborhood. But what if the zoning commission won't change the zoning, and land in the opposite direction got the new mall? Honestly, this is not where new investors should focus. It's the slowest possible trip around the flywheel as well.

Like all strategies there are ways to make money with land by improving it to be developed by someone else later, but it's not a best path to House FIRE in my opinion unless you have years of experience already or have insider information on upcoming developments. But insider information will give you an advantage on any real estate opportunity.

On the surface, **foreclosures** might seem like a great opportunity. And they are. Which means that you're competing with all the big sharks out there. Investors with lots of cash and lots of experience who make foreclosure investing their full-time profession are your competition. A little hard for a newbie to compete with.

This investment also requires a lot of cash. Offers on foreclosures with a mortgage are rarely accepted, and most of these properties come with a big rehab bill on top of the cost of acquisition. You'll be going to the courthouse and bidding in cash and often bidding blindly on many of these homes. You'd better be prepared.

Now trying to get a home before it hits auction is another move. It can take months, or even a year, to close on a pre-foreclosure or bank-owned home. This time lag means your sight-unseen house might be in even worse shape a few months down the line.

Honestly, it takes a few turns around the flywheel before I'd suggest even thinking about foreclosures. It's certainly doable, but really beyond the scope of this book. If you ever want to get into this, then I suggest putting in a good amount of time in stage one of the flywheel—knowledge. And then partner with someone with deep pockets.

The **rent to own** option might sound enticing. Rather than purchasing a property outright, you lease it from the owner, with a portion of your rent going toward the down payment. You put a little money down at first, and after a year or two, you can exercise your option to buy the property or not.

Honestly, this is a great deal—for the owner. It could be a great deal for you, too, if you're the one leasing the property to your tenant. Generally, though, the sale price is set at a premium, the portion of the rent that goes to the down payment is small, and the option consideration—the up-front money—is nonrefundable.

Stay away from this unless you're the owner already. It's not really real estate investing; it's buying a primary residence for yourself with very special and strict conditions. Something I'd recommend bouncing off a real estate agent before committing to just make sure you aren't getting taken advantage of. There are other ways for you to invest that will be more profitable.

But **not timeshares**. Although resort seminars can be eye-popping and persuasive, do not buy timeshares ever! Go to eBay right now and look up timeshares for sale and sort by price from low to high. Congrats, you have 10,000 timeshares to buy for a $1 each.

But even for a buck, they are still not worth it. Lenny bought one in his twenties, which is why he swears a lot and has nightmares of golf cart–led resort tours. Most of these timeshares have rental restrictions, very high annual maintenance fees, and they are next to impossible to get rid of. Imagine having a mortgage on something that you can't even sell for 100 pennies. This is the worst thing you can ever buy that is tangentially related to real estate.

Consider **commercial property**, but not now. If you're interested in industrial, office, apartment buildings, or retail space, then this isn't the book for you. That's the big leagues and requires big league knowledge and partners as well. Commercial property can be a smart investment, but one which you should grow into. For your first five properties stick with residential. Hell, it took me 300 trips around the flywheel before I ventured into commercial.

You probably have an intuitive understanding of how residential investing works. You've rented a home, maybe you've purchased a home and you may have fixed up a home. Like most homeowners or renters, you can look at a house and have some general idea of the costs involved and your expectations as landlord. You just have to match Lenny on his residential landlord bedside manner, and honestly that bar is really low.

However, the commercial investing flywheel is not the same as a residential investing flywheel. Everything from the lending process to the inspection process is different. Expectations in regard to property management and build-to-suit renovations are a different beast altogether. Plus commercial vacancies can take several years to fill. For someone potentially working on tight margins, this can get tough for a newbie.

8

"Okay, Alan, I'm ready to blaze a trail with my real estate investing. Shall we FIRE up the grill?"

Well, now that the unpleasantness is behind us, we can focus on the true meat of your real estate investing strategy sandwich—the juicy center of your investing roast. The Gordon Ramsay daily special.

Let's finally talk about what you should invest in. It's simple, it's whatever Alan Corey is hawking these days, duh. Go to his website at TheHouseOfAC.com and buy ten of everything. Then whatever is left over in your bank account, go buy a house.

For real, the reason real estate gurus like myself exist and "sell our secrets" is that we are obsessed with passive income. We want to wake up each day and think, man, that thing I did two months ago made me $3 yesterday and $10 today.

Or relish the fact that the house we bought three months ago just paid for the internet and electric bill today. And we naturally think, "Wow, in three years that house plus my book sales will probably cover all my federal fines for disturbing bald eagle eggs."

So, yes, the most cash flow addicted House FIRE heads will also naturally branch out to other channels to earn passive income wherever they can. We are looking for extra ways to make money in our sleep. The bed bugs don't bite us when we are making money while dreaming.

You always hear that if the real estate guru had such special information, why would they share their secrets? They really make their money teaching and not doing. And this is simply not true.

I honestly want you to make money in your ZZZs too. My motivation in life is teaching others how to do this, and I'm not worried it will eat into my profits one iota.

Why? Because, for one, most people will read this book and do nothing. They won't stick to buying a house in three months even though this book will give them every step on how to do it. It takes personal motivation and a belief in yourself to venture onto a new path. That can't be taught in a book, or a seminar, or a class.

Two, everything I have said in this book I have shared over hundreds of coffees, lunches, and happy hours with friends, clients, and Lennys, and I just don't have the time to keep doing it. So I've put my wisdom in a book and share it just to open up my calendar a bit. Let us help each other without ten texts back and forth on a time that works best.

And three, real estate is local, so what you do in your hometown will have no effect on what I'm doing in my hometown. If you do happen to live in my hometown, well, how come you haven't signed my online petition to put a statute of me in the town square? I know I wrote your email address on it perfectly. Is it because my statue has a ten-pack for abs? I don't see the big deal.

Regardless, even if you are my neighbor and won't sign my very necessary statue petition, I will still buy your real estate deal if it matches what I'm looking for and I'm pretty sure you will still buy my deal if it fits your investing criteria. I'm okay with this because there are enough deals to go around, and I can't physically buy them all. But enough about me. Let's get to chatting about what your personal product expertise in snooze-based income will be, because that's the crucial next step.

Essentially I have created six levels of what I want you to invest in, and these six levels begin from low and work up to high. The lower the level, the easier it is to get into the product but the less money you'll make overall. That's okay, though, not everybody can jump in right at the top or even the middle of the real estate investing hierarchy. For now, let's just identify your price range, and we can figure this out in more detail later.

You get in where you fit in. Just for the record, I started at the bottom. I worked my way up, gaining experience as I went.

Starting is the key. It's far more important *that* you start than *where* you start. Believe me, many people have made millions just at the level where they started. You can start low and master that level and become the best there is.

My strategy was and continues to be to try and move up a rung with each subsequent five purchases. After five spins, I usually feel comfortable leveling up. There's no right or wrong strategy here, but being an expert in a niche can pay huge dividends for you.

Now I should note that all of this stuff is highly location-specific. Different areas of the country, different population densities, and other factors are going to determine what products are available. There aren't a ton of studio apartments in rural areas and there aren't a lot of horse ranches in urban centers. Lenny frustrates many a real estate agent asking for these.

You're going to need to get familiar with your investing area and figure out what your best options are. Everybody has a different budget and skill set. That means acquiring as much knowledge as you can about the situation in your area.

Be prepared to get out of your comfort zone. You will need to expand yourself if you're going to expand your wealth. Fortunately, you have an advantage I didn't have when I first started: you have this book.

A property is considered more desirable if it offers more options. Product options are like having pivots in your investing strategies—the more the merrier. Some options may be these:

- You can rent it.
- You can renovate it.
- You can add square footage to it.
- You can change its use.
- You can up zone it to be higher density.
- You can down zone it to be lower density.
- You can rezone it to be a different use altogether.
- You can split it into two or more properties.
- You can combine it with a neighboring property, or assemble the properties, to create a bigger parcel of land.

No property will have all these options, for sure. The more options, the better, though, because a property with options gives you options as an investor as well. It gives you more flexibility to get the most out of the property.

Okay, so let's talk about these six rungs on the residential investing ladder.

Rung 1: Individual Condos/Coops/City Apartments

These do make great rentals, yet they have their problems. For one, they don't appreciate as well as other properties. Further, they come with hefty maintenance or HOA fees that can eat into your profits (HOA is homeowners association). They also have few options when it comes to expansion or combining, unless the neighboring unit is available for sale as well. The HOA itself can limit or change the rules governing short-term or long-term rentals at a moment's notice that can crimp any of your best-laid plans.

HOA boards are notorious for being a bunch of power-hungry Karens and Kyles. True story: Lenny once put "HOA President" on his online dating profile and even got the bots to stop spamming him.

With apartments, you're also limited in what sweat equity you can invest. Plumbing is often shared and can't be moved, working hours for renovation are limited, elevator access could be a problem for big jobs, and so on.

Also, the bedroom count is a bit wonky when compared to single family homes. For example, the more bedrooms, the better, if you're doing renovations and flipping since you are usually selling or renting to a family. You'll more easily sell a three-bedroom unit than a one-bedroom or studio.

On the other hand, though, I've found that when it comes to renting these types of properties, the fewer the bedrooms is sometimes better. That's because these are often rented by college students and other young adults. The more roommates, the more conflict, and the more likely you are to have trouble collecting rent.

It's not too hard for two roommates or a couple to get along and work things out. Three buddies exponentially increases the problem. It's hard for a tenant to find two friends that need a place at the same time, but it's not too hard to find one friend that needs a place at the same time (usually their current roommate and they just want a different place but still live together). Thus, a two-bedroom in these properties has always been my favorite.

Rung 2: Town Houses/Row Houses

These are similar to the last category. The difference is that you generally have more square footage to work with. Since these units are attached on at least one side, you can't really make them wider. However, you might be able to expand them out back or even turn a cellar space into a finished basement. If there's enough room, you could even convert an attic into a living space like a home office or nursery. These properties are still limited in options, but not as much as condos as you potentially have a yard or garage to help maximize value.

You still have HOA concerns and shared walls and roofs, but some investors prefer having the HOA in this situation because they cover the costs of fixing and replacing roofs and landscaping and take care of the amenities in the property. However, since all units are similar in size and shape, you are beholden to the lowest price town house in your community affecting your value. If you have one town house in the community that sold for $200,000 last week with its original furnishings, it's going to be hard to sell yours for $1 million even if you put $500,000 in renovations in it. Everyone will just want to buy the $200,000 one and put $500,000 in it themselves instead of paying you a $300,000 premium for it.

Rung 3: Single Family Properties

This is probably the most common for beginners to get into as it's the most available and common product type out there. There are a lot of options here for both short-term and long-term gains. Single family properties are abundant in the marketplace and appeal to the largest number of people.

Single family properties typically offer you the most number of options. You can buy and hold as is, possibly increase the footprint of a house, and potentially up zone it for increased and more valuable density if local zoning allows. This can be done by adding a stand-alone accessory dwelling unit, sometimes referred to as a mother-in-law suite, to have two properties on one lot. If not, you can usually build up or build out, or both, and make vast improvements.

You can potentially buy the empty lot next door and assemble the two parcels together to create a large plot of land for your single family. If that parcel is a higher-density residential lot or a commercial lot, you can even rezone your single family residential property to match the neighboring lot's zoning.

Single family properties can have a variety of strategies to exit from, but typically its best use is going to be to remain a single family. I just wanted to plant some seeds in your brain on how to look for treasure-hunting opportunities around each of your homes.

Downsides include being on the hook for all the expenses. You don't have an HOA to help offset the big ticket items, which means you are fully responsible for all repairs— expensive items like replacing roofs and fixing foundations, and replacing mechanicals like HVACs and hot water heaters will fall only to you.

You should budget for these repairs from day one, because they will happen. Pretty much everything in and around a home needs to be replaced every fifteen years. But if there is an emergency like a fire or other out-of-this-world damage, your home insurance should cover the repairs and you shouldn't be hit all at once for all calamities to go wrong entirely on your dime. A minimum budget of $100 a month per rental is recommended, and you can't go wrong budgeting a higher amount if you want to be on the safe side.

Rung 4: Vacation Rentals

These are single family units, condos, or town homes that you rent out by the week rather than by an annual lease. As such, they tend to bring in a lot more money. For example, if you owned a house on the beach in west central Florida—the Tampa Bay area, for example—you might rent it for $4,000 per month on a twelve-month lease. On the other hand, you might be able to get that every *week* from vacationers.

Sounds great, right? Well, there are a few downsides too. For one, you'll more than likely have to pay up to 30% of your revenue to a property management firm. This firm helps get you renters as well as takes care of the property since you may live in another state or far away. Further, depending on where you buy, you may only be able to get so many weeks of rent as vacation areas are seasonal. You just have to do some math and figure out what's right for you as well as understand what local city or HOA rules you'll have to follow.

Vacation areas may also be impacted the most by climate change with hurricanes, mud slides, fires, and more, and extra insurance requirements may be in store. Also, you may feel tempted to use the vacation home for personal use during the peak season, but this means you aren't pocketing as much cash. So instead you visit in the off-season, but it's not a fun time to use the house then. So it can be a bit of a catch-22 of an investment.

I've put it as a rung up from single family as this is typically a higher price point getting into, costs a little more to own and manage, and getting out should be a little easier since the location is killer, so it takes a little more experience in most cases to get into this world of investing.

Just note, this choice can be economy driven. If people don't have the budget to go on vacations, then you are going to have more vacancies than you typically might and that can be a painful hit until the economy turns around.

Rung 5: Small Multifamily (Duplexes, Triplexes, Fourplexes)

Remember back when I talked about strategies and mentioned how duplexes, triplexes, and even fourplexes were virtually identical to single family homes? That's because multifamily residential properties of under five units are thought of by the banks as single family homes. That makes them easier to finance, and they tend to provide more rent per square foot.

They are zoned for higher density and are typically near walkable commercial centers, making them in high-demand rental areas.

As explained earlier in the book, if you have four single family homes that are renting for $1,000 a month, it's always going to be better to get a fourplex instead that rents for $4,000 a month if they have the same purchase price. One vacancy doesn't hurt as much and expenses are going to be cheaper. You only have one roof, driveway, or foundation to replace instead of four. It's real estate investing at scale.

Now if you want to buy a primary residence and an investment property, a small multifamily allows you to mix primary-residence living with real estate investing and this mix has amazing benefits. Let's dig in.

If you are buying an investment property, a lender typically makes you have a down payment of 20 to 25%. But if you are buying a primary residence, you appear less risky to a bank, so they allow you to put down as little as 3% using something called an FHA loan (or 0% with a VA loan).

Okay, you are pretty savvy now, you've read half of *House FIRE*. Do you see where I'm going with this? You see the huge opportunity here?

Yes, you can really buy a small multifamily with a 3% down payment. All you have to do is live in one unit as your primary residence and rent out the other units in the building to offset or completely cover your mortgage. Imagine not having to come out of pocket to pay your mortgage payment because your tenants are covering it. Imagine how quickly you can save for another rental property.

Further, a bank will calculate the rental income you will be getting on this new property to actually allow you to buy a more expensive property than if you were just buying a single family home. They see it as extra income going to you, so the loan will be less risky; therefore, they will approve you for a loan larger than you thought would be otherwise possible.

This product type and loan combination is hands down the fastest way to use real estate as a path to FIRE. I know not everyone wants to live in a multifamily, but this is what I did as my second real estate purchase, and it completely changed my financial future. I actually cash flowed in my duplex, which means I was getting paid to live in my own home. This style of investing where you live in your own investment is referred to as house-hacking.

Rung 6: Commercial Residential

Commercial residential sounds funny, I know. Which one is it: commercial or residential? Well, this is the crème de la crème of residential real estate investing. We're talking about multifamily properties of five units and up, way up.

These investments are classified as commercial investments and need commercial loans, but the product type is residential apartments. These can be a cluster of garden-style apartment complexes, giant apartment buildings, even mixed-use buildings with storefronts on the ground floor and apartments on top.

So why is this such a great rung to be on?

Because in commercial residential, which I'll just shorten to apartments to make our lives, and by our lives, I mean my poor tortured typing fingers, easier, in these types of properties, income determines value. Let me explain.

Remember NOI? Net operating income? That's what's left after you subtract operating expenses from your rent. Well, in apartments, this figure is used to determine the actual cost of the property. I'm not going to dive into this too deeply here, as it really requires an entire area of study, yet I'll give you a quick example using our old buddy Lenny.

Lenny finds a twenty-unit apartment building with an annual NOI of $100,000. Now, the actual total rents come out to about $150,000, with $50K in annual expenses. Expenses include stuff like

- Maintenance
- Management
- Utilities
- Advertising and legal
- Vacancy
- Taxes and insurance

Yeah, property taxes and property insurance are legitimate apartment expenses. Okay, so with the $100K in NOI, the owners use a 10 cap and are asking $1 million for the property.

A cap, or capitalization rate, is a figure that's used to evaluate a commercial property. It's generally determined by market trend and comparative sales in the area. It's expressed as a percentage and is used like this: NOI/cap rate = purchase price. So in this example, $100K/10% = $1 million.

Why is that so good? Because it's the actual net income of the property that sets its resale value or cash-out refinance value. It's not based on what somebody *thinks* the property is worth. That's so often true with single and small multifamily homes as an appraiser determines value based on what a similar property nearby sold for. In these single family properties and small residential units, similar properties play a giant part in the price, and the income it may be generating is hardly evaluated. I'm not saying that there aren't some property comparisons in apartment appraisals, too, but it's far less as all they care about is the income.

For example, two duplexes side-by-side are the exact same in every way. You own one and your neighbor Lenny owns the other one. You are a more involved and informed landlord so you rent out your duplex for $1,250 a side, or $2,500 total. Lenny only gets $1,000 a side, or $2,000 total. Lenny wants to focus on his bowling league this year and is done being a landlord and sells the duplex to a House FIRE–focused buyer for $200,000. So what do you think your duplex is worth?

You make more rental income off yours, so it should be worth more, right? Unfortunately, your duplex is also valued at $200,000. Even though you get more rent, a residential appraiser will use the comp, or comparable property next door, to determine your value. It has the same square footage, built same year, has same finishes, so in their eyes, it is worth the same. I'm generalizing a bit, but this is the limitation of noncommercial properties. They are appraised mainly on sale prices of similar properties.

Commercial properties, on the other hand, are strictly appraised on the NOI. And these properties offer you the ability to easily cut expenses and increase rents. If I find a way to save $10 in the monthly water bill with low-flow shower heads, the property value goes up. If I increase someone's rent $20 a month, the property value goes up. You can build equity in these properties by decreasing expenses or increasing income. You can make improvements in a single unit to get better rent, start charging for parking, or build storage units in the basement for additional rent, and all that increases the NOI, and thus the value of your investment.

With single families and small multifamilies you will be limited to what your neighbor's house, duplex, triplex, or fourplex sold for regardless if yours is more energy efficient or if it gets more in rent. Apartments are just awesome because you control the value.

So what's the catch then? Well, you have to get commercial loans to purchase them, which means 25% down payment in most cases and interest rates are usually about 1 to 1.5% higher than residential loan rates. Commercial loans usually require you to refinance every five, seven, or ten years too. Plus you don't get the great tax breaks for living in the property like you would if you were house-hacking in a property four units or fewer. And your competition are Wall Street firms, well-heeled investors, and super savvy buyers. You don't see these guys in the smaller real estate space, so you can really be the king in a different product type as a mom-and-pop or small-time investor.

On the other hand, you can also buy commercial properties with a ton of partners much more easily. Even a group of thirty to fifty investors can pool their money and get a commercial loan. That wouldn't be possible on a residential purchase or with a residential mortgage.

So here we are again. Pick a combination of investing strategy and product type. Circle one in each column so you stay focused. If you aren't circling, you are going to get analysis paralysis later. And we are going to be picking up the pace.

Investing Strategy	Product Type
Buy + Hold	Apartment, condo
Fix + Flip	Town house
Fix + Hold	Single family
Hold + Fix	Vacation rental
	Small multifamily
	Commercial multifamily

At this point, I've covered the six rungs of residential real estate products, so let's now talk property class.

Property Classes

In real estate, properties of all types are divided into classes. There is no strict definition of property class and what constitutes a property to be in each level. It's mostly just marketing verbiage used by the listing agent to grade the property.

Starting at the top with A and ending at the bottom with D, these classes aren't always distinct or have a clear dividing line either, so it's usually a feel that you gain as an investor for what class a property is. For example, a low-end Class A might be virtually identical to a high-end Class B. Property classes mostly are representative of the tenant class, where each class has its own pros and cons and brings different returns to investors.

One thing to state up front, I have had amazing tenants at each property class, and I've had terrible tenants at each property class. But averaged out, you have fewer issues with repairs, turnovers, and late payment of rent in Class A properties than you do in Class D properties. And because of this, you have the classic risk-reward balance found in all investing.

Low-risk Class A means you make much less money for dealing with fewer headaches and issues, like investing in very conservative bonds. You make much more money in Class

D properties as you, or your property manager, have more headaches to deal with. You are buying very cheap properties with large cash flows, if you can keep them filled with tenants and the rent always comes in. If the neighborhood takes off, you win big. This is like investing in a tech start-up; you can have colossal returns with a little luck.

I'll break the classes down a little more to help you figure out which one you want to invest in.

Class A: These are the top of the line properties. Usually Class A neighborhoods have a majority of owner-occupant properties with a mix of luxury housing rented by tenants with high incomes like doctors, lawyers, and white-collar professionals. These properties might be second homes or luxury apartments or in the most desirable part of town. These are usually well preserved and taken good care of by the tenants. There's little risk here, as these are desirable properties and can always be sold, which we call liquid investments. Yet, as stated, they offer less reward than other property classes do as a rule.

I invested in Class A properties early on while I had a day job because I was self-managing my properties, and I didn't want the headache of high tenant turnover, and I was worried about having tenants that couldn't pay. All my tenants in these properties made salaries that were much higher than mine at my day job, so I felt safe doing it. Although it was a bit weird I owned the house they lived in, and they probably could afford to buy it if they had any interest in real estate. I was able to provide them a good home regardless of the income disparity.

I'm sure these high-class tenants looked at me as an idiot making things up on the spot and winging it every day just as I looked at them for being idiots for renting and not buying. It was a mutually idiotic relationship, which as long as there is balance, it should go well.

But when a repair did need to happen, my high-taste tenants had a higher bar of expectation. I couldn't cut corners or I'd lose them as tenants or reduce the value of my property. This was classic "investing where I wanted to live," and thus I got much lower returns on my investment.

I didn't cash flow very much, but got a lot of principal paydown. It was a safe, easy investment, and it taught me a lot about being a landlord with low risk and low reward. I eventually got the knowledge and confidence to branch out to other classes to get bigger returns.

I recommend skipping this property class if you want to avoid taking baby steps to House FIRE and you'd rather take the escalator, but like any niche, you can make it work for you with enough knowledge and experience.

Class B: Class B properties are still very nice, they just aren't luxury and not only for the rich. However, they still tend to be desired by highly paid blue-collar and white-collar workers because of the location. Maybe the neighborhood's defining feature is that it is close to a popular park or has public schools that are in high demand. The folks living in Class B properties require a certain level of quality that has to be maintained, but they aren't interested in high-end living.

Usually Class B properties were formerly Class A properties fifteen to twenty years earlier. They have just lost their shine a bit and don't have all the bells and whistles and trendy floor plans that the new luxury properties being built today have. Some of the furnishings are now dated, but not so dated to be a turnoff.

Class B property neighborhoods usually have a mix of primary homeowner occupiers and rentals, but are weighted more to owner-occupiers. This is good for building community as it's less transient, and a strong community usually means long and stable home values to come.

Getting into a Class B as an investor means you pay less for a property than you would in Class A and thus returns are slightly higher. Your investment is still liquid. You'll most likely sell to an owner-occupier trying to get in the neighborhood than selling to an investor, and this is a good thing. There are more owner-occupier buyers than investor buyers, and there are a lot of loan programs for these buyers to help buy this property from you.

You can do cosmetic updates prior to selling to add some value, but usually you don't have to do a major renovation to get top dollar either in rent or sale price.

Class C: This class is probably where you're going to have the best results as an investor. Typically these were built in the 1950s and 1960s with solid brick foundations, the standard building code then. These properties offer the best value since they have good bones and you can add value to them with renovations. These are classic BRRRR properties. You can typically make a Class C into a Class B to increase value, but it's nearly impossible to turn a Class C into a Class A as you are competing with new construction properties at that level.

Class C properties generally have a working-class tenant base maybe working paycheck to paycheck, so there could be a little more risk if tenants lose a job or their car breaks down and they can't pay rent for a month. But, on the other hand, this tenant type can also be a tenant for life as they may raise a family in your home or have extended family living nearby.

Interestingly Class B and Class C properties typically get the same amount in rent for the same type of property, but Class C properties are cheaper to buy. The difference in price is because maybe the neighborhood as a whole has more crime, the schools aren't as good, it's farther from transportation hubs, or Lenny opened up a sex shop next to a four season landscaping company known to host presidential press conferences. All in all, a Class C property usually is in a neighborhood where there are more renters than owner-occupiers, so it's a little more transient.

Class D: These are the low-end places that a lot of newbie investors are afraid to touch, but after investing here for a few years myself, it's one of my favorite places to put money.

While you can get into a property very cheap, you'll have a lot of maintenance, probably a lot of turnover, and are potentially going to have to deal with lower income tenants who might have poor credit. Remember you can also pay a property manager about 10% of the rental income to take care of these headaches for you.

Real big money can be made here by savvy investors because more risk means more reward. Government programs for revitalization often start with the most neglected areas first, so you can really benefit from a neighborhood turnaround. You get handsomely paid for your extra effort and willingness to invest here. On the other hand, you may never see the neighborhood change. Your end buyer will be another investor who will value the property based on the rent roll you were able to achieve.

One positive is that Class D building tenants may have credit vouchers or other government assistance to give landlords a guarantee that rent will be paid, and this is a great way to lower the risk in these areas. If you allow your property to be a part of this program, your tenant and, thus, your property comes with annual check-ins and house inspections and other criteria to keep everyone in line. These programs also dictate what the rent is going to be, and their rates are usually close to market rate and sometimes over market rate.

Many investors avoid Class D to not be labeled a slumlord. In reality, these frequent inspections and rental limits exist solely to prevent you from being a slumlord. I've found across all property classes, if you provide safe and decent housing, you will most likely attract nice and caring tenants in return.

The real estate billionaires of the world put a lot of money in this class of property as they buy over 100-unit apartment complexes getting rent with government assistance and then get a property manager to handle all the moving parts. These big hitters are willing to take the higher risk these properties bring to make triple the money that a Class A or B would make them. They invest Class A and B to preserve capital, and Class C and D to generate capital.

Again, there is no agreed upon definition of property class and there is no property class to avoid. You'll have different returns, different problems, and different successes based on where you decide to focus your efforts.

What Location Should You Invest In?

Before you finish this chapter and enjoy a well-deserved adult beverage, let's quickly touch on where you should look for your first five investments. As a rule of thumb, I recommend if possible that you not go any further than a forty-five-minute drive from your home. I know some markets are too expensive within this range, but if you can make it work, it will benefit you greatly.

Even forty-five minutes is pushing it to the edge for your first five. Why do I say that? Because by staying within a reasonable travel distance from an investment, you're not limiting yourself to showing the property on weekends only. If something needs to be attended to on a Tuesday, it's not a big deal to drive there.

Also, within your neighborhood or adjoining zip codes, you can quickly grow into an expert. You probably already know a lot about that market. You're familiar with the population, the job scene, the schools, and so forth. If you choose to invest farther away, you're going to have to learn an entirely new market. On top of that, travel will be an issue, and you'll end up paying others to do some of the work you would do yourself if the homes were in your own backyard.

So if possible stay within forty-five minutes of your home and become an expert. Believe me, there are typically plenty of deals in that wide of a geographic location for you to find five in five years.

But you can also be an expert away from home if you must, but narrow your criteria so you reach expert-level knowledge quickly. Maybe only look at properties that are walkable to a certain subway stop or commercial center. Or maybe you want one that is within a ten-minute drive to the biggest employer or military base in the town. You just have to narrow the search area to save yourself from information overload.

Remember, your first five properties aren't necessarily going to be your best five. This is your investing infancy, so stay close to the crib. You're in a learning process, going around that flywheel five times.

To help you understand the thrust of this chapter, you need to understand this: You can easily get analysis paralysis by looking at too many different product types, too many property classes, too many investing strategies, and too many locations. A lot of newbie investors get stuck spinning their wheels at this point. They make the mistake of comparing a Class A studio apartment, a buy and hold fifteen minutes away, with a Class C multifamily fix and flip four hours away.

It's comparing apples and oranges, ya know cuz them are different 'n' stuff!

However, if you were to look at five different Class C two-bedroom apartment condo buy and holds within a block of a popular subway stop, then one will jump out at you as a clear winner to buy. Which one will give you the most cash flow and principal paydown based on the listing price and expected rent amount you can get for it? Which has the best chance of appreciation? Does one provide infinite returns?

It's so much easier to evaluate properties if you narrow your focus and just become an expert in one particular combination of strategies, product type, property class, and location and make that your specialty. Don't waste your time or energy looking outside your focus.

I strongly recommend starting by only looking at one combination and own it. This is the greatest way to get to the confidence section of the flywheel. If you do this, the best deal will be screaming at you, "Buy me, buy me, buy me!"

Your time to action is reduced since you are not looking at every listing on the market. Rather, you are looking only at the listings that specifically fit your specialty. Instead of browsing a thousand new listings a week, you are looking at five. It's a much better use of your time as a real estate investor and will guarantee you closing on a deal within three months using this approach.

Think of it this way: Your roof gets blown off in a hurricane. Insurance is going to pay for it. Do you want a Ronnie the Roofer to fix your roof, or do you want a Hank the Handyman to fix your roof? Most will pick that expert that only does roofs. Sure that expert will charge more because he knows the most about roofs, but he will do a better job and also most likely make your roof last longer and survive the next hurricane.

A quick, cheap Band-Aid fix from Hank is not the best long-term strategy. So think of yourself as an expert in a specific combination. Experts will make more money since they know more about a niche than anyone else. Experts find the opportunities faster than anyone else too. Riches are definitely in the niches in growing your House FIRE investments.

Circle the combination from each column below that speaks to you right now. This is now your niche.

Investing Strategy	Product Type	Property Class	Location
Buy + Hold	Apartment condo	A	Within forty-five-minute drive
Fix + Flip	Town house	B	Limited to zip code(s)
Fix + Hold	Single family	C	Certain school district
Hold + Fix	Vacation rental	D	Walkable to X
	Small multifamily		
	Commercial multifamily		

Now you know what to look for, and you know what investment combo you want to go for, and you know your total monthly expenses you are looking to eventually kill. Now what?

9

"Hold my hand to the FIRE, Alan, cuz I just c-c-c-can't believe I'm actually doing this!"

I can believe you're doing this. It's not so difficult when you break down the approach. And it's easy to build confidence if Lenny, of all people, can succeed. Now that we've explored real estate investing in depth and looked at how money is made, the different types of strategies and the types of products available to you, we need to focus on each individual deal.

Remember when I mentioned long, long ago in a chapter far, far away about how, when you got your boots on the ground, you'd want to develop a team to help you out? Sure you do.

Well, it's at this stage of the game where you're going to want to start assembling your deal team.

Your team is going to consist of these people (or not):

- A real estate agent
- A mortgage broker
- A contractor
- A title attorney
- A property manager
- An insurance broker

All the team members except for a title attorney are going to be optional, but it's good to have a collection of highly skilled experts when the time comes. Honestly, you just have to identify one good team member. If you do that, they've already surrounded themselves with the other good members you need. They are successful already, and they probably achieved success with their contacts, so just piggyback off them. You just need to know one person who is an expert in your area who can introduce you to all the team members you need.

What's nice about building a team is that there are lots and lots of real estate professionals upon whom you can draw. Even better, because you're hyper-focused on a very specific investing tactic, it'll make it that much easier for you to find team members and for those team members to help you get the best deals.

What's going to be the more successful tactic: calling up a lender or a real estate agent or a contractor and saying, "Can you help me invest in real estate?" or calling them and asking, "Can you help me invest in fix and hold Class C small multifamily properties in zip code 30017?"

The latter is the much simpler yes or no and doesn't waste anyone's time. If it's a no, they will have a specific person they can refer you to. You'll get passed on quickly to the right person by using this detailed intro. An agent will say, "No, I only work single family residential, but you should talk to Alan Corey." Or a lender will say, "I don't do renovation loans, but talk to Alan Corey and find out what lender he uses." Or a contractor will say, "Alan Corey told you to call me? Man, that guy keeps me insanely busy. I love that dude!"

This specific combination you chose (property types and classes, investing strategies, in the last chapter) is exactly how real estate investors introduce themselves to each other. They want to identify and meet people in their same space all the time. This is not to identify and scrutinize competition, but because they want to buy and sell properties to and from those in the same space as they are.

Once you find someone else in your same investing niche, these people actually will become your great friends. You'll call them often to discuss shared tenants, shared contractors, or see if they have lending options or details on a certain property. It's actually kind of fun to nerd out with like-minded House FIRE maniacs. It is quite amazing, but by being specific in your criteria and telling others, then real estate leads start finding you.

If nerd matching is sounding difficult for you, find @TheHouseOfAC on social media sites to help connect with others. Now that I've got you talking the talk of House FIRE, let's teach you how to walk the walk.

This chapter focuses on what I like to call the 5 Cs of a real estate purchase. These 5 Cs apply to every deal you do and they are

- The catch,
- The cash,
- The contract,
- The critical review, and
- The closing.

Got that? Good luck in your investing.

Just kidding. I'm going to review each of these in detail. In fact, they're so important, each one is going to have its own chapter, starting with this one: the catch. Now, the reason I talked about teams before is that each of these Cs has its own team member or members, and I'll teach you how to spot a good agent shortly who will be your connector for building the rest of your team.

A savvy investor knows the value of their team and how to employ them and how using your team will help you zip around that flywheel even faster and with each spin a step closer to House FIRE. So let's cannonball right in: this chapter will be all about the catch.

The Catch

What's the catch? It's not a tricky kind of catch. This catch is a catch, a capture. In other words finding the house you want to buy. Catching and reeling in a big fish, or more accurately, a big property.

There are lots and lots of ways to find a home. However, one of the best ways is to find yourself a quality real estate agent who will work on your behalf to find you a deal. Now let me say outright that not just any old real estate agent will do. They're not all created equal, just as with any salesperson. The fact of the matter is that a lot of agents are what I like to call "umbrella salesmen."

When I lived in New York City, every time it rained, there were guys outside the subway station wearing rain ponchos and selling umbrellas. They were opportunist salesmen since they couldn't be found selling anything if it wasn't raining. And plus it drove me nuts they didn't even believe in their own product. They wore a poncho to stay dry, yet sold umbrellas.

Are all umbrella salesmen the same though? Sure they were licensed to sell umbrellas (potentially), but these guys aren't going to the know the nuances and differences between a rain umbrella, patio umbrella, and a sun umbrella. They are seasonal salesmen, only getting in the biz when it's typhoon or hurricane season and then switching to another profession during a drought.

Now I don't mean to insult anybody, yet, in my opinion, a good agent is a salesperson who can work year-round and has experience in your combination of investing. Their job is to help their client sell or buy a property in an active and proactive way.

Sadly, in my career, I've met plenty of real estate agents who believe that their job starts and ends with unlocking the door to a potential property and showing people around. Many times these umbrella salesmen-esque agents only got a license because the market was hot or because they got fired from their 9-to-5 job and being a real estate agent looked easy.

Well, that might work for personal home buyers on occasion, but not for us investors. What you're looking for on your first five properties is an agent who has gone through the flywheel personally at least five times.

I know, this might seem knit-picky, yet it is crucial. Consider that an agent who's invested in single family properties is probably not the best person to assist you in multifamily properties. Just as somebody who's purchased a couple of move-in-ready condos isn't going to have experience with flipping.

Yes, that will probably leave 20 or 30% of agents who are left after using these criteria. However, it's so worth the effort because you're going to find somebody who will become a partner for life. A skilled professional to help you build your empire. Someone who is going to make you an active investor, instead of just a knowledgeable investor that never buys a property.

Doesn't it make sense to find somebody to help you who has a bit more experience than you do? The answer is a qualified YES. I wish I'd thought of this during my first five.

In my case, I was actually teaching my agent. Now that I'm a licensed real estate agent myself, it's bonkers I get paid the same as another agent who has had their license for a week.

But what you're looking for here is somebody who has their own home and at least four investment properties under their belt. An agent who understands your needs as an investor. Of course, an agent that recommends this book to you is a good sign as well. Or tell them you are a House FIRE starter who wants to get going with [your specific combination]. If they know what you are talking about, you are starting in the right place.

Your agent not only acts as your inside person on the MLS, or the Multiple Listing Service that compiles all the houses currently for sale, but also they can help to guide and advise you. Since they have invested themselves, they are also going to be pitched off-market properties from other investors that they can pass on to you. Remember they will be talking to other people in the same combo space all the time.

Buyer's agents don't cost you any money (sellers of properties pay both agents), and they're a powerful tool to help you get around your flywheel as well. And they will be a connector for your other team members too. You'll appreciate having a real estate investing mentor as well as a real estate agent, and if both are free to use, then why not find a smart one.

And don't worry, an investment-savvy real estate agent is not going to steal all the good deals from you. There are plenty of deals this person sees each week, and they can't buy them all. If they help you grow your career with sound investments, they'll make plenty of money by making you successful.

Now, it's true that you're going to cut out the majority of umbrella salesmen, I mean agents, with your specific criteria, but it's worth the effort. You can find experienced investor buyers' agents in Facebook real estate investment groups at

The House of AC (www.facebook.com/thehouseofac) like I run, as well as on BiggerPockets.com and at local real estate investor meetings. All these hubs have real estate and FIRE desires like you so it's a good group to get to know, even if it is just virtually.

Find the right agent, and that agent will know a solid lender, savvy title attorney, and skilled contractor, and that agent will also recommend the absolute best real estate investing book to read! (If you are an agent reading this, that's me elbowing you in the ribs.)

Other Ways to Find Homes on Your Own

You're not limiting yourself only to your real estate agent, of course. You certainly should be looking for properties on your own too. Two heads are better than one. Also, as you find prospective deals, you can show them to your chosen agent for his or her evaluation and recommendation.

Here are a few ways for you to root out properties:

- MLS data collection websites such as Realtor.com and Zillow.com
- Real estate investing (REI) discussion forums and meetups
- People rooted in the community—neighbors, mail carriers, teachers, and so on—when you tell them what combination you're looking for
- Searching obituaries online and attending random funerals with a pocketful of business cards (This is a joke, don't be scummy.)

Once you get through your first three properties, there are more advanced options to choose from for properties four and five. I don't recommend these advanced methods until you go around the flywheel at least three times. They're considered advanced for a reason, and it's still a smart idea to bring an agent in to help you evaluate something you find. Some of these advanced options include

- Tracking down the owners of abandoned houses,
- Using tax records to track down absentee owners, and
- Connecting with property wholesalers who flip contracts, not homes.

Talking to your shared-combination nerds will connect you with these communities local to your area. You can easily be taken advantage of here if you're not careful. However, if something falls into your lap, you should certainly take a look. I'll even offer to take a look with you. I'll examine deals posted on my The House of AC Facebook and Reddit groups.

What're You Trying to Catch?

How do you know you've found the right house? Does it fit your investment strategy? Will it really meet your needs? Will it get you around the REI Flywheel? Does it get you closer to FIRE?

Depending on which of the four strategies you choose, you can employ some formulas to help you answer some of these questions.

Buy-and-hold catch criteria: This one is really all about the rental income a property generates and the purchase price. The basic formula here is: Monthly rent/purchase price = percent.

Of course, depending on your market, product type, and product class, these percentages will vary. You can see something as high as 3.5% in Class D to as low as 0.1% in Class A—not a good number. A lot will affect this, and, of course, the higher the percentage, the better cash flow you get. But figure out what your forty-five-minute radius offers or other location criteria in the current market and aim for the higher side of the average.

Example 1:

$1,000 monthly rental income/$100,000 purchase price = 1%

Pretty decent. If you, or our pal Lenny, bought this house with $20,000 down, that would mean an annual return of about 60% ($12,000 rent collected/$20,000 down payment).

Example 2:

$1,500 monthly rental income/$300,000 purchase price = 0.5%

Hmmm, that means if you put $60K down on this one, your annual $18K only gives you about a 30% return. This is a gross return, remember.

At first glance, example #1 is better since it has better cash flow. But example #2 just might be at a lower percentage as it's in a higher property class, or an area with a greater chance of appreciation. Maybe it's rented at or below market rates, or it has better schools.

But if you are always comparing apples to apples, you'll know a bad deal, average deal, and a good deal when you run the same formula on all of them. They will probably be all 0.5% and one is 0.6%. Or they are all 1% and one is 1.2%. These are just back-of-envelope measures, so you can never completely rule in or rule out a property using this formula, but it's a basic rule of thumb to use when first starting out.

Fix-and-flip catch criteria: In this strategy, it's all about the ARV. Remember when we brushed on this earlier? ARV stands for after-rehab value. This is the number that comprises the foundation of every flip you do. This is the number that tells you the minimum amount you need to sell the fixed-up property in order to cover all of your expenses, including your minimum profit. These costs include

- Purchase price,
- Cost of repairs including material and labor,
- Holding costs, and
- Minimum profit amount.

Whenever you evaluate a potential flip, you need to have a very good idea of these factors. You may not know everything up front, not until you actually visit the property and inspect it, yet you can fill in a couple of these blanks even before you talk to the seller for the first time. You'll get better at estimating each trip through the flywheel, of course. And bring a contractor with you to firm up rehab numbers if you can.

Aside from your minimum profit figure, which you can establish anytime, a good rule of thumb might be $10,000, but it can be less or more. The thing of it is, you don't want to lower your profit too far or you won't make much money. On the other hand, if you set it too high, you're going to find it hard to move on any deals. Being greedy might mean the flywheel never completes a spin and your path to House FIRE never begins. We don't want that. We have a three-month deadline set for you to get your first spin.

After this number, though, the first task is to run comps in the neighborhoods you're looking to buy in. A comp is a comparative sales analysis. You can do this yourself by taking the address of the property and plugging it into Zillow or other real estate websites and see what sold nearby that was similar in size and condition.

You're trying to find recent sales in the area of homes that match the one you're looking at—homes that match what your rehabbed home will look like. Similar quality, similar size, and within a block or two. This will give you an idea of what you can expect to sell your fixed-up property for.

Note, this is also where to ask a quality real estate agent to assist you. Especially somebody who's gone around the fix-and-flip flywheel a couple of times. They have access to the MLS to help you generate comps in a much quicker and professional fashion.

Let's take a look at a quickie example using ol' Lenny the Landlord. What we know is that Lenny now has decided that he won't do any flip unless he can profit by $15,000. Lenny has found two houses fairly close together that he's considering.

House #1	House #2
Asking price: $85,000	Asking price: $96,000
Comps show a potential sales price of about $125,000.	Comps show a potential sales price of $150,000.

The first property has a spread of $40K and the second $54K. When you subtract Lenny's minimum profit amount, that spread goes to $25K and $39K, respectively.

At first glance, we see that house #2 seems to be a better choice. There's more room to wiggle, right? Well, after looking at the two houses, Lenny discovers that house #1 only needs about $10K in cosmetic repairs to bring it up to the level of quality that the comps sold for. Assuming a ninety-day turnaround and other costs, Lenny gets an ARV of $120K.

House #2 needs about $35K worth of work. When Lenny factors in the other costs, he gets an ARV of $150K exactly.

Both can work, yet house #1 offers Lenny the better advantage because after buying, holding, and fixing it, and factoring in $15K in profit, he's still got a nice comfy $5K cushion to work with. That cushion allows him to sell at a little bit of a discount if he wants to sell more quickly.

On the other hand, the second house *has* to be sold at or even above market. This could be trouble. There are always delays, extra costs, and other unanticipated events that crop up. Lenny could barely break even or even lose money on this deal.

The choice is clear for Lenny.

Fix-and-hold catch criteria: The formula for this strategy is similar to the buy-and-hold formula, with one important exception. In this scenario, we're not just buying a rental. We're talking about buying a fixer-upper and fixing it up and then renting it. So the formula you want to use here is this one: Monthly rent/(Purchase price + rehab costs) = percent.

So if you found a house for $100K and that house needs $25K worth of work before you can rent it for $1,300 per month, you'd plug those figures into your formula like so: $1,300/($100K + $25K) = 1.04%.

Not bad, really. That works out well. Assuming a 20% down payment, you're in for $45K. This house gives you a pretax, pre-debt service cash return of 34%. Of course you then have to factor in maintenance, debt service, and other stuff, but you're still looking at something in the range of 8 to 10% cash-on-cash return after expenses.

Cash-on-cash return is a really good metric, as it bases the return of the cash you put into the deal, not on the return of the deal itself. For example, if you put in $10,000 on a deal that earns you $100 a month, that is better than putting in $50,000 on a deal that returns you $125 a month. The deal level has $25 higher returns, but at the cash level, you spent one-fifth less to get almost similar returns, and therefore much much better return on your money.

If you really want to juice your cash-on-cash return, you can also try to cash-out refinance and try to get your $25k renovation budget back and part of your down payment too.

Hold-and-fix catch criteria: This one is a little more complex because it combines strategies 1 and 2. In this case, you're buying a house and renting it. Then after a while, you're going to flip it. So you need to figure out both your annual cash-on-cash return as well as the eventual ARV. So here we use two formulas: Monthly rent/Purchase price = percent.

You know that one already. If it works out well, this property makes a decent rental. However, you've got to look into the future and figure out your ARV: Comps – purchase price + fix-up costs + additional costs + profit = ARV.

This strategy is a bit tougher because it forces you to try to predict the future. How long will you hold the house? What might the market be like a year or two down the line? Which pivot or exit will you implement? In this scenario, you have to be profiting while you hold the house, and that's not really negotiable. If, for example, your ARV gets a little tight down the road, this can be offset a bit by the profits you're making from rent.

If stuck on what to do with a property, then sometimes it makes sense to clearly identify your House FIRE goal with each property to buy. Do you need $15,000 more to buy a triplex next to the park? Okay, let's find a way to make $15,000 on a flip and sale or with a cash-out refi. Or do you need $300 to cover your car lease payment? Okay, let's turn this property into your automobile payment fund and find a way to make $300 in cash flow out of it.

Maybe you need to raise $1,000 to fly a "Lenny Is a Creeper" banner off the back of the airplane around town? Well, then, the cash can be made up in a flip maybe with installing a little higher end appliances to sell for a higher price or with maybe a year's worth of cash flow by attracting a higher end rental tenant. Whenever you can identify what you want the money for usually helps quickly settle any debate on what approach to use on your investments and that keeps the flywheel spinnin'.

10

"Alan, umm, how the hell do I pay for these things without burning through money?"

The last chapter looked at the first C of the 5 Cs of a real estate purchase. This chapter is all about the cash, the second C.

It takes FIRE to make FIRE, right? Or is it money to make money? Either way, of all the topics surrounding real estate investing, money is obviously the most important to most folks and to those who just skipped ahead to this chapter, well, I don't blame you. Not everyone is Lenny with endless amounts of investment capital, but maybe if you did read the first nine chapters you'd have an idea how Lenny got so much cash in the first place.

Any who, let's carry on to the age-old question: Where does the cash to invest in real estate come from?

I'll get to that in a bit. Sorry, for the bait and switch. Let's first cover something else that is probably on your mind and then I will get to that cash stuff. First, how should you buy the property? By that I mean do you buy a property in your personal name, in a corporation name like an LLC, or do you just trade four railroads and a utility company for Boardwalk and Park Place? (Yes, you make that trade.)

For your first five properties I recommend that you simply buy all your rental properties in your own name. The biggest reason is that when you buy property in your name, even if your name is Lenny Costco Ramsey, you tend to get better interest rates and often a larger LTV (loan to value) threshold, meaning you can buy a rental with a smaller down payment. So with the property title and loan in your name, you save money on both purchase and holding costs.

Oh, also not just the mortgage payment is higher when you buy in an LLC name. The landlord utility bills are in a company name, and that can come with higher rates. The insurance has to be in a company name and that means higher rates. Plus LLC tax returns are going to be more expensive and more time consuming for you to have to file separately, and we are looking to save both time and money to get around that flywheel.

But, but, but what if I get sued? Isn't an LLC going to protect me because LLC is short for limited liability company after all? If something happens in one of your properties owned by your LLC and you get sued, it's the LLC that gets sued and not you. That is correct. The tenant can't come after you personally for liability damages and that's a good thing. But an LLC is not ironclad and there are still ways to come after a landlord personally.

However, you can buy a simple personal umbrella liability policy from your insurance company that covers you here, and it's much cheaper than LLC insurance. Also, if you do buy a property in an LLC, everything needs to run though that LLC account. You can't have your rental home insurance payments auto-deduct from your personal checking account or you can't use a credit card in your name to buy supplies one time for your rental or you are piercing the corporate veil and you lose your liability protection anyway. It's all or nothing when you are an LLC, so be careful if you go this route.

I'd say, though, that by the time you start getting to your tenth deal, you definitely should look into tax entities and how to structure your investing business using them or if you are buying properties over $1 million, then LLC is probably the way to go.

But for your first five rentals, focus on the deal instead of the LLC. It'll be faster trips around the flywheel each time, and it's much cheaper to not do this for now. And note, you can always switch a property via a quit claim deed for about $150 from your personal name to an LLC after you buy the property if you change your mind down the road. And waiting gives you plenty of time to come up with a creative business name like House FIRE Here I Come, LLC (doing business as Killing Bills Like a Mofo in Retirement).

Fine. Let's talk cash now. The truth of the matter is that, yes, it does take cash to invest.

If you are looking for your most basic entry point to House FIRE (so you can be financially independent and retire early, which is the goal here), that will come with either (a) having money saved up and earmarked to be spent on a house, or (b) finding a deal so sweet you can't stop thinking about it and you figure out the money later.

Maybe you already have a decent amount of savings from your prior FIRE endeavors, and of course this can be used. The good news is if you have a down payment saved up, getting the money to pay for the rest can be found in a dizzying variety of other places. Alternatively, if you don't have the money, but you find a good deal on a house, then the money will not be hard to raise.

I like to save up in $10,000 chunks. When I first got started, I used $10,000 to put 10% down payment on a $100,000 place. It was a one-bedroom condo that I creatively turned into a two-bedroom and got a roommate to pay $750 a month, which covered most of my mortgage payment.

For my second, third, and fourth properties I didn't have all the funds to do deals on my own, but I found deals I knew were going to be profitable. So I found partners with money and I found contractors with time. This combination allowed me to spin around the flywheel faster than trying to do it all myself (all spelled out in my first book). I could either do nothing and make nothing, or do something and get a small slice of a big profitable pie using partners.

For the record, profit pie ranks first of all pies, followed by blueberry pie, and then shepherd's pie.

You will have so many loan options from banks and mortgage lenders salivating to give you money if you find a deal. What makes a good deal though? Money folks—those investors and lenders you find with your combination-criteria intro—always have an appetite for low risk and good returns on an investment project. If you can show in a spreadsheet why your deal meets these criteria, then they will jump on board. It usually also takes experience, so just know each property you acquire will be easier to raise money for.

You've already learned why it's better to leverage and not buy properties in all cash. You've learned how to size up a deal as well. So being the deal-finding guy or gal shouldn't be too much of a stretch for you now. And I'll chat more about this in the next chapter.

Before I get into this list of loan options to help you out, though, I think it's a good idea to talk preparation. As you no doubt already know, success is 80% preparation, 15% luck, three garlic cloves, and a tablespoon of donkey sweat.

It's important in all seriousness that anytime you go to a bank and ask to borrow money that you be prepared. Prepared to answer their questions and show certain documents so that they're comfortable handing over giant bags of cash. It's the polite thing to do.

Real estate is best when the majority of it is leveraged. Paying all cash limits your deductions and greatly magnifies your tax liability. Never buy real estate with cash.

There is one exception, however, and that exception comes with a caveat. The only time you should pay cash, if you have it, is to win a bidding war on a really, really great property. And only if you can close fast and get a discount. Then you refinance it later and get your cash back and you put a mortgage on the property.

Cash is king, so if somebody wants $100K for a house and you can offer cash and close in seven days with no due diligence, go for it, but you should be offering $90K because it's cash and it's a fast close.

Honestly, though, try to avoid paying cash at all costs, at least for your first few properties.

What to Have Ready for a Lender

There are quite a few types of lenders out there. I'll get into the different ones in a few moments, but no matter who you're asking, these are the documents you would be wise to have already prepared as part of your loan package. Like comedian Bob Hope said, "A bank is a place that will lend you money if you can prove that you don't need it."

Last two years of your tax returns: Any entrepreneurs out there will already be painfully aware of this requirement. If you're self-employed, then these serve as proof of income. Yet even if you're not, showing a two-year history of your income gives the lender a sound picture of your financial situation.

Two months of bank statements: This gives a more recent snapshot of your financial picture. It also shows the bank/hard-money people that whatever cash you claim to have has been in your possession for a little while. What they don't like to see is a savings balance of $237.50 in March and then in April you suddenly have the $25,000 you're using as your down payment.

Last two pay stubs: No shocker here, right? Shows proof of employment, if you're employed, and shows how much you earn. Also the stubs have to be issued within the last four weeks and not four years ago. You aren't going to pull any fast ones on a mortgage lender.

Credit check: This isn't something you have to prepare ahead of time. Nowadays, banks and just about anybody can run a credit check online in seconds. Just be prepared for this. It wouldn't be a bad idea for you to run your own credit a few months prior to applying for a loan. This will give you an idea of where you stand and time to fix any errors.

And don't worry about having multiple credit checks from different banks if you are loan shopping or talking to different lenders as multiple credit checks by different banks over a forty-five-day period only count as one check overall and don't hurt your credit score. The myth that a credit check is going to greatly impact your credit score is overhyped; if anything, you want to always know where you stand at all times.

A property's income statements: If you're buying a property that's already rented, then you can use the income from that property to help you qualify for a loan. This is most definitely the case for big multifamily but can also be the case for a single family home.

If you're buying a house that currently rents for $1,750 per month and you can show proof of income through the lease and seller's rental receipts, this is huge. Potentially an appraiser will use recent rental comps in an appraisal if the property is vacant. This will help you show the bank how you're going to pay off their loan with this rental income proving their risk to loan you money is very low.

This rental counts as part of your income and thus lowers your debt to income ratio and reduces the risk to the lender. If a bank sees there is $1,750 in rental income coming in and your mortgage payment, insurance, and taxes equals $1,250, then why wouldn't they give you a loan?

Your third-grade report card: I hope you got good marks in Ms. Brown's class that year because a bank is a nosy little fucker, and they are going to ask for everything ever mailed to your house with your name and social security number on it. Underwriters are trying to prove why this loan you want will not fail, and you have to pass all their annoying petulant tests, just like you had to do in third grade. Although they won't actually ask for academic records, it will feel like it. Just play along. They are giving you a lot of cheap money and assessing the risk of the property you are investing in, and it's worth the hassle in the end.

Lender Options

Okay, let's take a look at different lender options now.

Mortgage brokers: If you're on your first trip around the flywheel, then I strongly recommend going this route. Mortgage brokers are a flexible asset because they offer the largest number of possibilities. For example, if you walk into a bank and ask to get a loan, they're going to offer you only the mortgage products they currently have available at that moment in time. A mortgage broker, on the other hand, works with dozens or even hundreds of different banks.

They can offer you any number of options as well as some unconventional ones too.

I've personally had this work out well for me. I once went into my bank and asked about their loans. Then I went to a mortgage broker and had them talk to the same chain bank I was in earlier, and the mortgage broker found me a better deal on the same package.

Because brokers deal in high volume and with multiple lenders, they can often find you a loan that's better than anything you'll find on your own. I personally use the mortgage broker JasmineTeam.com for my loans—both for my personal loans and my investment properties. Team leader Jasmine Krnjetin is an investor herself and gets the business side. She's the expert I recommend if you want a key member with a few flywheel spins on your lending team.

Mortgage loans are typically fifteen-year fixed or thirty-year fixed, meaning your monthly payments and payoff period are calculated over a fifteen- or thirty-year period and won't change. Which is better?

Well, if you want more cash flow, then a thirty year is your friend since payments are going to be much lower. If you want more equity and principal paydown, then a fifteen year is better. My default House FIRE advice is take the thirty-year loan. Due to inflation, money is worth more today than it will be worth tomorrow (remember the ice cream cone?), so you'll want extra cash in your pocket today more than extra cash in your pocket tomorrow.

I do occasionally recommend a fifteen-year loan if you want to buy a rental property to pay for college. Buying a rental property with a fifteen-year fixed-rate loan after a child is born instead of parking money in a 529 College Savings Plan is a smart way to invest. This strategy would mean the house is paid off by the time the genius child heads off to chug beers and smoke joints in their first dorm room.

This fully cash-flowing property should cover the majority or all of their tuition costs with potentially some extra money for a decent supply of weed. (Not my college experience, but maybe one that you want for your children.) And then once that child graduates, that house is still spitting off money for the second child to go through college. So with about $25,000 (down payment on a $100,000 property) and waiting fifteen years, you can pay for endless children to go to college and get them high at the same time.

If you don't plan to own the property for this long of a time horizon, then a three-, five-, or seven-year ARM (adjustable rate mortgage) may be the best approach. These typically have lower interest rates than fixed-rate loans and then they adjust over the length of the loan. They still have a thirty-year payoff, the year amount in the name is just how long before they do their first adjustment on interest rate.

Depending on the market, they can adjust up and start to cost you more each month or the rate can adjust down and save you some money without having to do a refinance. But these ARM loans spelled doom for many investors during the last real estate crash, so use sparingly.

What are the different loan options you can get? Let's start with the loan options for primary-residence buyers. I start here because you can acquire a property as your main home, live in it for a year, and then go out and buy a new primary home. This is the twelve-month cycle I mentioned before, or a smart way to buy five homes in five years. You just make your old house a rental each time you move out, and the loan you got to purchase the house stays in place with the same terms.

FHA loans: The Federal Housing Administration has offered home buyers loans for a long time now. Their loans are potentially easy to get, on one hand, because they only require a 3.5% down payment. On the other hand, they're picky about the price and the quality of the home, be it a single family, duplex, triplex, or fourplex.

FHA requires owner-occupancy for the first year, so you can't get this low a down payment on a property you have no intention of living in. I mentioned earlier in the book that buying a multifamily (four units or fewer) and living in one unit and using an FHA loan to fund 96.5% of it is one of the fastest paths to House FIRE. Nickname-giving podcaster Brandon Turner calls this living arrangement house-hacking. It's now a common strategy among new investors.

After living in the house for a year, you can either choose to remain there or move out, keep the loan as is, and rent out your old space. This is how you can buy investment property for little down and quickly be an expert in the small multifamily niche.

VA loans: These are similar to the FHA in that they're fairly easy to qualify for. Of course, you or somebody on the title has to be or have been a member of the military. The VA loan is a little bit more flexible than the FHA, so it's worth looking into.

The bonus? You can actually buy a primary residence or a small multifamily with 0% down. That's right, zero down payment. There are a lot of fees that go with securing this loan, but it really opens doors quickly for you without having to save a ton of money. Talk about a free house. Lenny approves.

Doctor loans: If you are a doctor, there are great benefits to being a real estate investor. As high-income earners, you'll want a tax shelter to help defray the costs of high taxes. Banks really like doctors, too, not because they are busy healing the sick or trying to resurrect dead tissue. Nope, banks really like their high income and job security, even though most also have giant student loan balances.

The result? Banks will offer 0% down loans to doctors and physicians for primary-residence living as well. As a doctor, you can get a 0% loan for your primary and then put other money you might have saved for a down payment into an investment property. Or live in a place for a year and then rent it out and go find a new primary. You get a thumbs-up from Lenny with either of these approaches (but can you check out that lump on it?).

203K renovation loan: This option is also offered by the FHA. This is a loan that encompasses the purchase price as well as the cost of rehabbing a property. It's a great way to get into a fixer-upper and have a little help with the rehab costs.

The interest rates are low, and the same 3.5% down payment can be done. However, you have to be an owner-occupier as well. You also have to hire a licensed contractor and can't do the work yourself. However, again, if you're planning to buy, fix, and hold, it could be the right opening.

Talk to a mortgage broker and your real estate agent to explore your best options and strategies around this. It's a little tricky and can be a slow-moving process to get approved and get an offer accepted, but if you can pull it off, all the better. Having someone pay 96.5% of your rehab cost is a pretty amazing deal.

Conventional loans: This is one of the biggest categories your mortgage broker will find for you. With a standard loan package, you'll have to put a down payment ranging from 5 to 25% and pay private mortgage insurance for anything less than a 20% down payment. This is what most people use to buy a primary residence and is considered the typical loan.

Jumbo loans: A jumbo mortgage is much the same as a regular conventional mortgage, just bigger. Fannie Mae and Freddie Mac (federal mortgage associations) set conforming limits on how large a mortgage can be in the country to get the best rates. This helps stabilize the housing market (theoretically) and allows more people to qualify for loans.

The exact number of this jumbo limit depends on what state you live in. Basically, anything under about $510K is a conforming mortgage except in higher priced areas. Anything over that is a jumbo loan. They're much the same and they may have a slightly higher rate since the loan is bigger.

Reverse mortgage: The reverse mortgage has become more popular over the last few years. It is, in a very real sense, an easy way to pull equity from your property without having to pay it back, at least not right away.

Essentially, you apply for a reverse mortgage and get a lump sum or scheduled payments to you each month based on the equity you have at the time. When you sell or die, the beneficiary of your home has to pay back the old reverse mortgage or refinance it into their own name.

There are some stipulations, however. First, you generally have to have 50% or more equity in your home. You also have to be sixty-two years old or older. For a means of generating capital from a primary residence, though, this can be a great way to get some fast cash without having to repay it immediately. A savvy planner could use these payments as a way to House FIRE and live their best life right before heading into the afterlife. You can be a baller with a walker, a geriatric version of a pimp with a cane, if you play your cards right.

Investment Loan Options

Maybe you already own a house and don't want to move into a new property yourself. You are just interested in a regular ol' investment property. Where do you get cash then? You aren't interested in creative financing. I hear ya. Let's go over your investment options in that scenario.

Home equity lines of credit (HELOCs): Let's look at your primary residence. It's valued at $400,000 and you have a $100,000 mortgage on it. You can access that $300,000 of equity through a home equity line of credit. A bank would provide you access to 75% of that, or $225,000. You can write checks using this equity as collateral.

Lenny does this all the time with excellent results, and he only pays interest on what he accessed. So if he writes a check for $10,000, he pays interest on just $10,000. If he spends $50,000 of his HELOC, then he pays interest on that $50K until he pays it back in full with a house sale. It's like a credit card in that way. If you don't use it, then you don't pay anything. If you spend it on stupid stuff, well, you have a stupid bill to pay each month.

Braggadocios time from yours truly! This method helped me get my biggest win in real estate by getting me a "free" million-dollar house. Ears perking up? Thought so.

So I, too, had $300,000 available to me in a HELOC on my primary residence due to a way-too-favorable appraisal I got. Like a smart man looking for cash, I didn't question it. The bank overvalued my house to my benefit and then gave me a HELOC based on that overvaluation.

I used the entire $300,000 I now had access to as a 30% down payment on a $1 million already renovated duplex three doors down from me in Brooklyn, New York. The bank loaned me the other $700,000 via a traditional conventional loan. Let's look at the numbers:

- $300,000 HELOC for down payment was "free," but once I used it, it cost me $1,600 a month at 5% interest until I paid it back.

- $700,000 mortgage from bank cost me $4,750 a month at 7% interest for a thirty-year fixed.

- Total amount I had to pay was $6,350 a month after taxes and insurance, but I rented the duplex out for $8,350.

- I now made $2,000 a month just by using my untapped equity in my home that was doing nothing for me (plus tax breaks, principal paydown, yadda yadda yadda).

Oh, so what makes this my best win ever in real estate besides the obvious benefits in getting a free cash-flowing million-dollar duplex? Oh, I did absolutely zero renovations and sold that building four years later for $2 million to a celebrity with more money than sense. Due to lottery ticket rapid appreciation in Brooklyn that I didn't factor in or anticipate, I made $1 million profit with $0 invested of actual cash—it was 100% financed. Now that's how you do it, Lenny. But even without that appreciation, my buy-and-hold plan of earning $2,000 a month on a free duplex would have suited me just fine as well.

Now be careful here. As with any cash generator that comes from your personal residence, you are putting your primary home at risk. You need to understand that. But HELOCs are a great option to access equity if you are house rich, cash poor, and find yourself looking at a can't-miss investment opportunity.

Self-directed IRAs: Look into converting your IRA into a self-directed IRA or starting a self-directed IRA. Instead of your traditional IRA or Roth IRA that limits investing in stocks, bonds, and mutual funds, there are steps for you to self-direct or self-invest in instruments of your choice— like real estate. You get additional tax breaks from investing within a retirement account, but you can't touch the money to spend on yourself until you are 59.5 years old though. A still rather youngish FIRE age.

Hard-money loans: Hard-money loans are private loans made by individuals, groups, or even businesses. As the name suggests, the terms of these loans are going to be a bit steeper than your standard commercial options. People instantly relate hard-money with the mafia, and, well, that's definitely one way to invest in real estate. Especially, if you like deep ocean office meetings.

Hard-money lenders are also non-mafia people who want to earn passive income on their cash. Additionally, they're also very much concerned with the exit strategy you have on a property. In short, they want to put their money in something, make a beautiful dollar while it lasts, and get their seed money back as quickly as possible.

You can find hard-money lenders advertising in every real estate investing group. Your real estate agent probably has legitimate recommendations to hard-money lenders as well.

You're not likely to find any hard-money loans that are made for more than three years. They tend to be very short term, high interest, and often come with a balloon, or a full repayment of principal due at the end. For example: Suppose Lenny wants to buy a $180,000 run-down duplex. The bank says they aren't going to lend on it because Lenny is a little too overleveraged because he just left his full-time job to Barista FIRE.

Lenny asks a hard-money guy he knows to lend him the cash for 90% of the total purchase and rehab, for a total of $200,000 investment. The hard-money lender agrees and says he'll lend the money at three points, and 15% interest, and a one-year balloon payment. Essentially, this is a super expensive loan. Breakdown here:

- $20,000 of Lenny's money for down payment
- $180,000 borrowed ($160,000 to purchase and $20,000 to renovate)
- 3 points is 3% of the loan as an up-front fee to hard-money guy for a cost of $5,400
- Mortgage payment of $2,300 a month
- Balloon means you have to pay it off and refinance it in one year

Lenny looks at this and realizes the hard-money lender is going to make $33,000 off him for one year. Lenny is only going to make $20,000 on this investment in a year.

Some would stop here and say, wait a minute, Lenny is doing all the work fixing it up and not making as much money as the hard-money lender. He should walk away.

But Lenny looks at it differently. He looks at this deal as being able to almost double his money in twelve months, turn his $20,000 down payment plus $5,400 in fees into a $40,000 payday after he fixes up the property and refinances it (or sells it). He wouldn't be able to do this without a hard-money lender willing to provide flexible terms to him, and that flexibility has a price.

This is a creative way to get into a long-term investment when banks aren't willing to lend to you. Also, the more success you have with a hard-money lender, it's not uncommon for the fees to get cheaper over time as you build some trust with them.

11

"So that last chapter was for people with money. I really have no money burning a hole in my pocket to do this, Alan."

Lemme continue to tick off the 5 Cs, and this C is still about the cash portion with an additional chapter because I know not everyone has cash. We all have to start somewhere.

Let's discuss how you can buy real estate with absolutely no money to your name. And no money doesn't mean easy money. It's quite the opposite—the less money you put into the deal, the more you have to work for it. You have to work to find a deal that will be profitable, work to find a seller who will get creative, and work to find partners to join you. Some options other investors and I use with very little of our own money are listed next.

Subject to: "Subject to" investing is finding an owner who wants out of their house by any means necessary.

Typically this works best with a for-sale-by-owner situation or a very experienced title attorney or real estate agent holding your hand. Your offer is "subject to" you taking over their mortgage payments.

Maybe you can't qualify for a loan on your own, or you don't have enough down payment to make the numbers work, so you make an offer on the property that says, basically, "Let's keep the mortgage in your name, but I'll make the payments. If I miss a payment, the property becomes yours again. If I don't, I'll continue to make payments until it is paid off."

Or maybe you negotiate to refinance the property into your own name in a few years when you know you'll qualify for financing. It's whatever creates a win-win scenario for both of you.

Owner or seller financing: This is a workable option if you're looking at a property and you find out the seller doesn't have a mortgage on it. And bonus, the seller is having a tough time selling it. Maybe she's an absentee landlord and lives in another state. Maybe she inherited the property and doesn't want to deal with it. With owner financing, essentially, you're making the seller of the property your hard-money lender.

There are an infinite number of ways to structure this sort of deal. Let's use Lenny's example from the last chapter when he bought his hard-money deal. Maybe Lenny this time could offer 0% down payment, so he can acquire the property for free, borrow $20,000 on repairs from a partner, and still have a one-year balloon agreement with the seller. Maybe there are no points and he can save himself $5,400 in up-front fees. Maybe it's the same terms but only a 5% interest rate to reduce carrying costs.

A seller is way more motivated to get the home sold than a hard-money lender is to lend you money, thus the terms are going to be much more favorable from a seller-lender.

At the end of the day, Lenny gets the seller to agree to zero down payment, no points, 3% interest rate, and a six-month balloon payment. So as long as Lenny can get the work done, he can refinance in six months and come out way ahead than if he went the hard-money route. The seller got the price she wanted, plus an additional six months of note payments, and she got her duplex sold. So win-win all around and both sides feel like they got a good deal.

You can take this to the extreme. Most banks have a limit that the smallest mortgage they can do is $50,000. It's a federal law limiting banks to this, not that they are wanting to avoid helping out people at this price point. The law stems from the notion that expenses and fees cannot be more than a certain percentage of a loan, and $50,000 is the threshold that gets you to that minimum percentage.

So this limited scenario occurred with a retiring investor about an hour away from my house. He had a fifty-home portfolio where each home was worth $40,000 and were rented out for $500 each. He could sell them to cash buyers only since lenders wouldn't lend on them. Or he could sell them as a package to someone with a hard-money loan or commercial loan. But hard-money is short term and even commercial banks want $50,000 or above value on each property so they can resell the loan to another bank down the road if they want.

So I offered the retiring investor to take them all if he seller-financed it. He thought it over and eventually agreed with a 10% down payment, 7% interest rate, and a fifteen-year term. I couldn't get a loan at a bank for these terms, and even if I could, they'd want 20% down payment minimum. Seller financing was the only way he could sell them unless a cash buyer was around. It was a win-win for both parties.

I imagine I could have bartered the seller down to a 0% or 5% down payment in exchange for a higher interest rate if I wanted to, but, instead, I took his terms and negotiated down the price per house to $30,000 each. This saved me $50,000 in down payment money I had to bring to the table. The new $1.5 million purchase price, instead of the asking $2 million purchase price, meant I had to bring $150,000 to the table to acquire the properties.

I ran the numbers and with a professional property manager in place to handle this crazy workload on my behalf meant I'd be cash flowing about $50 on each property. So my $2,500 in new monthly cash flow would be nice, but in fifteen years when the seller note is paid off, it will be $25,000 a month. That's more than halfway to HELLFIRE. And I imagine there will be some rental bumps in there so my tenants will want to stay, so it might be closer to $35,000 a month.

Now if I don't want to wait for the cash flow in fifteen years, then my option is to push property values up to $50,000 each so a bank will lend on them. Say I budget $7,000 to get an extra $10,000 in value on each one. That's an additional $350,000 in money out of pocket ($7,000 x 50 homes) to do that and that would bring my total to $500,000 of my own money on this one deal. Or instead of finding $350,000 in the short term, I could take $7,500 in cash flow that the entire portfolio kicks off every three months and reinvest it into renovating one property at a time.

However, if I did either a short-term BRRRR or a long-term BRRRR with this renovation idea, I could do a cash-out refinance at a bank once complete. A bank will lend on 75% of the new value. So assuming fifty homes get to a new $50,000 value each, that's a total value of $2.5 million, which a bank would give me a loan amount of $1,875,000 on. Most likely that loan will have a lower interest rate than what I'm currently paying the seller, so even though the loan balance is higher, the payment each month will be the same.

This refinance would pay off the current seller-financed loan of $1,350,000 and that means I take back home a

$525,000 check for the difference. Remember, I put $500,000 total in this deal so I got all my money back plus $25k. Infinite return time.

What remains are fifty homes on a new higher bank note balance but with a lower interest rate. Those homes will still be cash flowing me $50 each, or $2,500 a month. Oh, and I still have $625,000 of equity in them ($12,500 in equity per house x 50 houses).

What to do? Sit back and cash flow like crazy in fifteen years or cash out a windfall now? It sure is fun making House FIRE decisions, isn't it?

Partnerships and joint ventures: I just want to touch on this again quickly. The concept of real estate investing partners is a big one and deserves its own book, honestly. However, it's possible to put together a group of people to pool their cash and experience to make up the down payment to purchase an investment.

For a seasoned investor, this is a good way to get a partial ownership of a property yourself without having to put up any cash and using other people's money to acquire properties you couldn't have gotten just by yourself.

Here's what I mean as a basic example: Lenny wants to buy a twenty-unit apartment building. The building has an NOI of $100K and is being sold at a 10 cap, making the purchase price $1 million. Lenny can get a commercial loan for $750K but needs $250K as a down payment, and he is Lean FIRE with no income and trapped to living within his budget.

So what Lenny does is gather five friends or business contacts, each with $50K to invest. Lenny states that each partner will get a 17% ownership in the property. Lenny, because he's putting together and managing the deal, takes a 15% ownership as payment for his contribution of knowledge. He doesn't have money to put in, but he's happy to take on the extra effort to source and manage this deal due to his early retirement and open schedule.

A $750K loan runs about $50,000 per year, and taxes and insurance add another $15,000 in expenses, leaving a positive cash flow of $35,000. Each of his investors gets a nice $5,950 annual return or an ROI of 11.9% before taxes. They don't have to worry about management of the property, and they get a share in all income, tax breaks, and equity buildup. In a nutshell, there are lots of people out there who like these kinds of deals, and Lenny gets ownership in a building for his sweat equity, rather than his money.

The kicker is all these investors are now going to say, "Good job, Lenny, go find another one." And Lenny continues getting free pie slices of real estate ownership.

Borrowing from friends and family: It could be that you have family members with money they'd like to invest. Naturally, as I mentioned early on, sometimes these people are your biggest detractors only because they know you and feel that if they can't then you can't either.

However, once you go around the flywheel a few times without them, they may begin to change their tune once they see that you're prospering and know your stuff. What makes this a good source for cash is that there's no need for following SEC guidelines because you have a preestablished relationship. However, I caution you not to try this one until you have gone around your flywheel at least twice because you really want to know your stuff before managing other people's money. You want to be extra careful with money from family and friends because if the deal goes sideways, so can your relationships.

Wholesaling: This is another interesting way to get into real estate with no money. In wholesaling, you're not actually buying anything. What you are, in truth, is a dealer in assignable contracts. However, you will learn quickly about cold calling, negotiations, and contracts as well as deal analysis. Let me show you a quick example of how wholesaling can work.

Let's suppose that Lenny wants to get into investing but has no cash to speak of. However, Lenny does know a few flippers who are always on the lookout for a good deal. One day, Lenny comes across an off-market fixer-upper and goes to see the property to see if they would be interested in selling it. After talking with the sellers and doing a little analysis, Lenny figures that maybe one of his flippers might want the property for the right price.

The sellers say they would sell him the house off-market for $75K. The house needs $50K of work to bring it up to par with the neighborhood. Similar houses in the neighborhood in good shape are selling for $140K. Lenny happens to know a flipper looking for a deal like this who insists on making at least $10K on every deal.

So Lenny negotiates with the seller and gets the house under contract, an assignable contract, for $70K. He then goes to his friend and says that he'll let the house go to him for $80K. The friend looks at Lenny's analysis and agrees and takes over the purchase agreement.

Lenny has just made a nice $10K for finding, negotiating, and then assigning a contract on a home to his friend and it didn't cost him a dime! Well, in reality, there's some work involved in advertising, networking, and the like, yet wholesaling can be another way to get started without having big piles of cash. Doing a few deals like this can build up enough capital to move you up to the next rung. You learn a lot about evaluating properties quickly this way, and you build relationships with other investors. It's a great first step for newbies.

Rent-hacking: Remember house-hacking I mentioned earlier? If not, house-hacking is purchasing a primary residence and using the benefits of a primary-residence loan to acquire a property. And then you make money by renting out your spare bedrooms to cover your mortgage payment or renting out the additional units if you purchased a small multifamily, which we discovered is a way to make money.

What if you don't have 3.5% down payment for a house? Well, have you ever heard the term rent-hacking? Pay attention because I taught many a beginner on how to do it to save for their first down payment on a house down the road.

You're not buying anything here. The idea is to find a place with more bedrooms than you need to live in and negotiate a reasonable lease price with your landlord. Maybe get a steep discount for a two- or three-year lease or for paying a few months of rent payments up front if you have that handy.

You want a place you can afford on your own and just have your name on the lease with the ability to sublease the spare bedrooms. Then to succeed you find roommates willing to rent by the room or you get Airbnb guests in your spare rooms to cover the majority or all of your rent payment.

An example would be renting a four-bedroom for $2,500 a month, but you live in the smallest bedroom. You sublet the master bedroom for $1,000 and two secondary bedrooms for $750 each. Boom, you just got rid of your own lease payment and you get to live for free in your own home. Go sock away that $2,500 lease payment you would have had into a savings account, and in ten months you'll have $25,000 as a down payment on a new place to purchase.

I know this works as I've had tenants do it to me. One even rented all three units of a triplex from me and then Airbnb'd them all out. She was making more than what I was charging her. It didn't last more than a year, though, as I just started Airbnb'ing it myself for the extra cash, but I give her kudos for finding income-producing ways as a nonproperty-owning "rentlord."

12

"Call the FIRE department, Alan, because I don't want to lose this catch!"

We've explored the first two concepts of the 5 Cs—the catch and the cash—so let's pause and spend a few minutes on the idea of actually putting a property under contract, the third C. This secures your find and makes it yours.

Now, just sending an offer isn't the end of getting a deal. Other steps need to happen to get a seller to accept your offer. You can accomplish this with bribery, or money laundering, or tax evasion. All these strategies work really well if you are looking to invest in a 6- x 8-foot cage.

If you have designs on a place that offers a little bit more freedom to its tenants, then keep on reading. In this chapter, I'm going to look at the components of a purchase and sale agreement and what you need to know about each. A real estate agent or attorney really is your best ally in the nuances of your state's contract on a home purchase, but I'll provide you with a general overview.

As an investor you need to know how to make an offer strong without just raising the purchase price. There is a fine balance between getting a great deal under contract and losing a deal to someone else by trying to be too greedy. And this third C is where you are really becoming active on the flywheel and you start to earn your chef hat.

I've honed the art of getting my offer accepted over my twenty years in real estate investing without paying the most for the property, and I'll share my tips with you because I trust you with these secrets of the game. In return, just don't use these tactics against me if we are bidding on the same house. I will never forgive you, but will admire your style. If it happens, just know that it's me who is toilet papering your trees.

To craft an offer that wins, you just have to understand all the levers you can pull within a contract to make a strong offer overall. *Overall* is the key word here. Sure, purchase price is a giant factor in getting an offer accepted, but other levers make your offer stronger without raising the purchase price. To do this you have to fully understand some key real estate lingo, which I've outlined here for you.

Earnest money (or escrow money): Lever one is earnest money. When a seller accepts your offer and signs the purchase agreement, the house isn't yours. This is only the preliminary step to the actual transfer of the property. A contract is, in lay terms, a binding agreement to buy and sell the property, and both parties are going to put their best foot forward to achieve just that.

Because this isn't a 100% guarantee that you'll actually be buying the house, the seller needs a little something to act as security. That's where earnest money, or escrow money, comes into play. Earnest money is a deposit, usually refundable, that a third party holds as a way to get some of the buyer's skin in the game. Remember, the seller is taking their property off the market to give you a chance to close on it, so they need an incentive from you to show you have every intention to buy the property.

If you follow through with the contract, then your earnest money gets applied to your down payment amount that a bank will require from you. However, if you try to get out of buying a home for reasons not allowed in the contract, you forfeit this money to the seller for wasting their time.

I will cover in a bit the legal reasons a buyer can back out of a contract and get their earnest money back. But for now, I just recommend only going under contract on something you have every intention of buying.

You've probably seen or heard of sellers taking multiple offers. While this is a way to give them a backup plan, the offer they signed, yours, is the only one that counts until you back out of the contract. So earnest money, which varies depending on the deal—anywhere from $500 to 5% of the purchase price is not uncommon—and is held by a third party is just what it is, a security deposit.

A bigger earnest money deposit on your offer naturally makes your offer look better than offers from other buyers with lower earnest money amounts. So pulling this lever and upping your earnest money deposit makes you look like a more serious buyer and someone who really wants the house. It's also no skin off your back as all the money goes back to you as long as you close on the property or back out of the contract via the outs allowed within.

We'll look at Lenny's offer on a hot property where he pulls this lever to win out in a bidding war at the end of the chapter, but let's explore the other levers in an offer first.

Critical review: This is the time, after the offer is accepted, for you to inspect the property and make sure that it meets your expectations. This is also sometimes referred to as your

172 | HOUSE FIRE

due diligence period. More detail on this in the next chapter when I cover the critical review, which is the fourth C.

Just know this due diligence period, usually around one to four weeks, allows a buyer to learn more about the home and then back out of the contract if it was not up to snuff and get their earnest money back. Maybe you found another house you like better; maybe the inspection went poorly; or maybe you searched the address in Google Maps and found the neighbor naked and passed out on the lawn. Of course, depending on the attractiveness of the neighbor, this can be a pro or con.

As a buyer, you must use this time wisely to find out everything you ever wanted to know about the house. You can review leases with the property (which automatically transfer to the new owners with the same terms). You get the house inspected by a professional inspector. You can bring a contractor by to get quotes for work you plan to do. Whatever further information you need about a house, this is the time to do it.

You'll never want to spend the time testing each faucet and electrical outlet before you submit an offer. Instead, you submit an offer with the understanding these are working, and then if you find out later during the inspection period they aren't, you renegotiate the contract. So that's the time to do the real critical review and why you've baked this one week to thirty-day time period into your contract.

The shorter the due diligence time period, the more lever pulling you are doing to really accelerate your offer to the top of the pile.

Appraisal contingency: A bank won't lend you money on a property without doing an appraisal first. I'm not saying they don't trust you, but if they are giving you money to buy a place for $500,000, they want to make sure the property is actually worth $500,000. Typically this can take fifteen to twenty-one days to get an appraisal done. If the house gets appraised for lower, you can renegotiate the contract or back out of the contract and get your earnest money back.

On the other hand, if the appraisal comes in higher than purchase price, then you just shut your mouth and don't say anything. You are buying the house at a discount and you aren't obligated to share the appraisal value with the seller.

Now you can lever pull by removing this contingency entirely and really having an attractive offer. You are saying, basically, I'm going to buy this house no matter what an appraiser thinks it is worth. The risk, though, is if it comes back with a $475,000 appraisal, then you have to bring an extra $25,000 to the closing table or you can decide to walk away and forfeit your earnest money.

Financing contingency: This is basically a contingency that says you will get approved for a loan within fifteen to thirty days. If you do, then you will move forward with closing. If you don't, then you, the buyer, get your earnest money back. If you are already prequalified from a bank or buying in cash because it's a hot market, you can remove this contingency if you think you'll get a loan no matter what happens.

A bank usually issues a prequalification letter that you can attach with your offer saying you should have no problem with getting approved for a loan up to a certain amount. The letter is dated, so you might get denied for a loan after the contingency ends (you lose your job, for example) and then in that case the seller does get your earnest money deposit because it happened after the contingency deadline.

Closing date: This one is self-explanatory. This is the actual date that you'll sit down across the table from the seller and get carpal tunnel from signing all of those papers. This is the day that you'll officially take possession of the property. If you are buying a vacant home, then sellers are usually motivated to close as fast as possible. A closing attorney typically needs a week minimum to get your paperwork in order.

If it's occupied, the sellers may still be looking for their next home and would appreciate a longer close time. It's always good to ask what works best for the sellers and then try to match it.

So now Lenny has his eye on a renovated Class A single family home in a good school district that you happen to own. Let's imagine you get three offers on it. Which one stands out to you the most?

	Lanny's Offer	Loony's Offer	Lenny's Offer
Purchase Price	$350,000	$360,000	$340,000
Earnest Money Deposit	$1,000	$500	$10,000
Due Diligence Period	30 days	21 days	3 days
Appraisal Period	30 days	21 days	0 days/ Cash offer
Financing Period	30 days	21 days	0 days/ Cash offer
Closing Date	60 days	30 days	10 days

If your home is vacant or you are under contract on your next home but need to sell this one first, then the quick close date in Lenny's offer is going to be attractive to you. Not to mention, Lenny more or less has only three days to back out of the contract or he's going to forfeit $10,000 in earnest money. You'll know quickly if this deal is going to close or not.

If Lenny doesn't close, these other two offers are probably still interested in the property on the same terms they offered just a week and half earlier and would most likely be open to being a backup offer for you. If you do choose Lenny, then you can see how he gets the house without having the highest offer. He used levers in other areas to bring his offer to the top.

Now, if your kids are in school for one more month, you might like Loony's offer the best. It's much more money and gives you flexibility on having to move out without disrupting the school year.

If you have no idea what you are going to buy next and you prefer not to be rushed, you may be attracted to Lanny's extended closing date offer. The due diligence is lengthy, so it will drag out time for Lanny to look for problems with the home, look at other homes he may like better, or self-invite himself to drunk nudist neighbor soirees. Extended due diligence can be risky business for sure.

Now that's all for the third C, the contract phrase, let's see where we go from here. You still have the critical review and the closing. No one said this stuff moves fast.

13

"Alan, am I ready to set this house on FIRE?"

Well, here we go! You've clattered up to the top of that first big hill on the roller coaster and you're poised on the top, just waiting for the big drop. But you're not quite past the point of no return. In other words, you've made an offer on a house and it was accepted. Now what?

Once a seller has accepted your offer, you are in the due diligence phase as it starts immediately. This kicks off the fourth C, the critical review stage. Presumably you've already done some kind of preliminary analysis on your investment returns and have made the decision to buy because you want to House FIRE (to be financially independent and retire early).

If this property is going to kill one of your bills, now it's time to make sure the property is what you expect it to be.

This is where you have a home inspection done, review the leases if any, bring a contractor by to estimate repairs, do a thorough walk through, and, well, be a nosy little fucker. In this chapter, I'll go through each component so that you have an idea what to expect and what your options are.

The lender: Obviously, the big task you're doing now is getting your financing in order if you are using borrowed funds in some way to get the house. You've probably already prequalified, but you still have to get the actual loan. This is where you need to sit down with your lender and get the real numbers, down to the dollars and cents.

- Exactly what will the monthly payment be?
- How much will your property taxes come out to?
- How much will the insurance cost?
- What are the final closing costs expected to be?

Home inspection report: Go into this knowing that you should take the results of a home inspection report with a grain of salt. Remember that no house is going to be 100% perfect. Even a brand new million-dollar home is going to have some issues. An older home will have more. It's natural. No home is perfect.

Home inspection reports are extremely critical and are designed to be scary. Just remember that, as a buyer, you're not the one who's supposed to be scared. If there are glaring issues, you can certainly address them, of course. However, an inspection report is meant to help give you leverage in a renegotiation.

If an inspection report comes back with issues that you didn't know about when you made your offer, then you can negotiate with the seller on that basis as long as you are still in your critical review period of due diligence time. You can even pull out of the deal if it's something really major and get your earnest money back.

But in my experience, a seller will fix most major problems because if you back out, they will have to disclose the problem to the next buyer. And that buyer will ask for it to be addressed also or walk away. And the next. And the next. The owner will have a difficult time selling the home unless they remedy the issue or greatly reduce the price of the home.

Generally, though, if you've checked out the property thoroughly with a real estate agent before making an offer, your inspection report will allow you to ask for a reduced price or to have the seller fix the most pressing issues before the closing. Keep something in mind, though. The market will determine how much negotiating power you have.

If the market is strong (let's say it's a seller's market), then the seller may not wiggle very much. They'll probably have multiple backup offers and may or may not be as flexible even on some larger inspection issues. And, again, there is no perfect house, so don't expect a seller to ever be willing to fix everything found in an inspection report.

Negotiating based on inspections: Here's an important tip. If your inspection reveals something that needs fixing, something that requires a professional in other words, then get an actual quote. If you can go to the seller and show them what the inspection report says and provide them with an exact quote to fix it, this can strengthen your position.

There are two things you'll possibly get from this situation. First, the seller will give you a credit and lower the purchase price. For example, if your inspector says that the HVAC duct system needs replacing and you have a quote for $6,000, the seller may simply lower the purchase price by that amount. But what if you don't have $6,000 extra to pay for it and you'd prefer cash?

You can also set up a cash-at-close situation where you still pay the initial price but you get the seller to cover $6,000 in some of the closing costs to buy the house (your attorney fees, mortgage fees, government recording fees, for example). I'll cover the costs to close at the end of the chapter, but just know the buyer usually pays all closing costs, yet this can always be negotiated.

In a way, getting $6,000 in credit from a seller in closing costs is better than the seller fixing items. It's better because it allows you to control how the issues are handled. If the seller agrees to fix it themselves, then they're going to do whatever they want. You have no say or control over this. Think about their position. Is it in their best interest to get the work done at a higher quality or go with the lowest bidder?

Stuff to watch for: The inspection report will probably come back with a lot of nitpicky items. A loose seal on the back door, a squeaky garage door, a broken ceiling fan, or maybe a dead body in the basement. These are items you can let slide, but here are a few things you want to know and that you need to address one way or another:

- Water issues: damage or leaks or rainwater getting in
- Mold: means there are water issues
- Asbestos: remnants of unsafe building practices
- Foundations: cracks, leaning, or settling
- Roof: damage, softness, or age
- Dead body in basement: frozen or buried, either way, get it removed

Now, there is no problem that money can't solve in a house. I'm not scared of anything I just mentioned, but I'd be scared of paying for it. The big problems are typically your five most expensive repairs you'll have to deal with on any home. I don't mind handling the fixes on these if I can get the seller to give me credit to match the quote I have from a professional.

Check out the lease: If you're buying a property that's already rented, then you should look at it as if you're getting a brand new tenant. Read through the lease that's in place very carefully and watch for anything that could be an issue for you. Additionally, ask to see the last three months of rental receipts as well to make sure the tenant is current on payments.

A lease transfers with the sale of the home, and you have to honor the agreements in place, so just know what the current landlord and tenant have agreed to. If it's not in writing, it's not enforceable. Tenants love to share handshake agreements they had with their prior landlords after a sale of a property, and I'd say half of them are bullshit. You just say it wasn't in the lease and you therefore can't honor it.

Buying as-is: An as-is sale can be a great way to get into a property at a discount. However, as the name suggests, you don't have the option to request repairs or to lower the price. The responsibility is on you to make sure the property meets your standards and that any issues are known to you before making an offer.

Now there may be some caveats here. For example, you may agree to buy a property as-is with the qualification that you get a home inspection report that shows no major hidden flaws. Things you can't determine for yourself such as foundation or roof issues, hidden fire damage and so on. Just keep in mind, though, that as-is condition pretty much makes everything your responsibility.

No matter what you're buying, you have to accept the fact that you're not going to know everything about a property. Even a home inspection isn't 100% comprehensive. They can't open walls and look behind cabinets. There is some risk, as with any endeavor. However, if you perform a careful due diligence, you will generally be in the driver's seat.

What you learn after the offer is accepted allows you to negotiate or even back out of a deal. You don't have to accept anything major that you don't want to. That's why the contract has stipulations built in. But if you are planning a major renovation and buying a fixer-upper that obviously needs some love, an as-is purchase is usually standard.

Things to Know about Budgeting

Let's peel back the curtain a little more on loans and other post-purchase issues before moving on to the next C. You probably know some of this if you've purchased your own home, but I think it's worth mentioning anyway since you are investing and not just making a primary-residence purchase. Your House FIRE goals will be affected on every purchase, so it's really good to understand the costs of buying rentals.

PITI: Most conventional bank loans have four parts that make up the loan payment. The first is **principal**: the amount of the actual money borrowed you're paying back. Then there's the **interest**, which represents a high percentage of the payment when the loan is new and a lower percentage as it matures.

Most lenders also include the payment of property **taxes** as well as homeowner's **insurance** in their payment. This is so that they are certain that their loan isn't going to be put in jeopardy should you fail to pay either of these on your own.

I like having the banks handle my insurance and taxes so I have a fixed monthly payment each month. When the insurance and taxes are collected, they go into an escrow account. This is a non-interest bearing account that's used as a simple piggy bank for the lender and is drawn upon when property taxes and insurance premiums are due.

You've also probably heard of PMI—private mortgage insurance. This is an extra small bit of money you pay when putting less than 20% down. It's a small insurance policy to the bank so that in case you default, they don't lose as much money.

This will probably not be an issue for most of your investments, though, as most lenders require a minimum of 20% down. But these are all items to discuss and will add up to be your total monthly mortgage payment if you are house-hacking or planning to live in the investment property for the first year and then move out and rent it.

Property management: Your retirement life may not be one with visions of dealing with tenants and plumbers. Well, guess what? You get a property at a good enough price or hold it for enough time to increase cash flow, then you can afford a property manager. And the more properties you acquire, the more money you will have to afford one and the quicker you do that, the more time you will have on your hands. And the more time you have on your hands, the more likely you are to write glib and loquacious real estate books.

Whether you hire a property manager or do it yourself, it's a good practice to account for these fees when doing your property analysis. You may want to switch to a property manager in due time, and it's good to have a budget for it. Should you choose an actual property management firm, they'll charge you a percentage of the rent or some other preset fee. The good news is that these fees tend to go down with volume—usually with five properties or more. This discount is the reason I like to scale to five homes in order to get the most out of House FIRE-ing.

A property manager usually doesn't get excited about managing one property. It's a lot of work onboarding a new owner and having to reconcile books and accounting for one home and one person each month. So you get charged accordingly. A property manager typically could charge 10% of the rental income a property generates. That way they are incentivized to keep the property filled and at the highest price possible.

However, if you have five rentals, the job is a little easier. They can scale their own efforts and consolidate the accounting a bit, and they usually will offer a discount. They'll charge 7 to 8% of rental income to manage. And if you have ten properties or more, well, you can negotiate them down to 5 to 7% in many cases.

Of course all markets vary, but if you scale your buy and holds, you can scale down expenses. Typically you can get a similar discount with lawn care providers, pest control vendors, and more once you hit the magic number of five properties.

Maintenance: Again, this is a cost you subtract when calculating your NOI (net operating income). You might set aside $100 for a single family home. Now you might say that $100 per month doesn't seem like much. What happens if you have a big repair? Well, every month that $100 goes into the bank and you'll have plenty of months of no repairs. Over time, your expense budget will add up and help to defray your costs on the big ticket items.

If the house you are buying is older or has some obvious deferred maintenance, then budget $200 a month and work that into your calculations. Yes, sometimes insurance will cover some of the major issues too, so you have a bit of a safety net. However, it's still a good idea to have something up your sleeve when you need it.

You'll get better at estimating this with each trip around your flywheel, but every home has maintenance, and it's just safe to budget for it from day one, but $100 a door (or unit) is a decent starting estimate.

Closing costs: I talked about this earlier, and yup we all hate these. Yet every real estate sale comes with closing costs. These are costs associated with the transfer of a property from the seller to the buyer. They include items like these:

- Title search
- Attorney's fees

- Mortgage lender commissions
- Appraisals
- Prepaid property taxes
- Prepaid home insurance

These items are just the cost of doing business and should be factored in on each purchase. You can get a precise number from your lender during the due diligence period on what it will cost you outside of the down payment amount, but I usually calculate 3% of the purchase price as a back-of-the-envelope estimate for closing costs.

To recap, during the critical review you are just doing a little more investigating on the property with hiring a home inspector or bringing in a contractor so you can identify immediate and future repairs. Maybe a paranormal investigator tells you to sage the home or burn it down after purchase. You just have to weigh all the information you get from all sources.

Further, you take this time to firm up your expenses from the lender to actually purchase the house, and then you double-check the ongoing expenses you'll have as a landlord once you actually own the property. This is supposed to be a money-making venture after all.

Don't sweat it, you'll most likely have a real estate agent and lender to help you all through this period and hold your hand and your sweet friends whom you met that invest in the same categories as you. This may feel like a lot to you, as a first flywheel spin, but it becomes easy breezy by the fifth time around. And believe it or not, the trip around the wheel eventually becomes enjoyable. You'll no doubt eventually invite your friends to ride along with you. And maybe even write a book to encourage others too. (I heard that's a side effect.)

Okay, got all that? Now that we've made the offer, got it under contract, secured the cash, and completed the critical review, let's move on to the last C, the closing.

14

"Hey, Alan, open the garage doors because you actually got me driving into my own FIRE house!"

In a stroke of absolutely brilliant irony, this chapter is going to be short and sweet, unlike the subject of same.

Everything is fast, fast, fast, until the actual closing. This is it, though, the culmination of all your efforts. You're about to make a complete circuit around your flywheel. It's time to sit down across from the seller and get yourself a nice case of carpal tunnel and do a FIRE dance as we have reached the last of the 5 Cs with the closing (to recap: catch, cash, contract, critical review, closing).

Assuming all the inspections went well, as did the negotiations, the title search from the closing attorney, the neighbors passed the clothing-optional test, and the other stuff that goes into this remaining few final hours, you're going to meet with the seller at the title company's office to handle the close. By now, you've already seen all of the documents that you've previously signed electronically, but you're going to see them all in person once again printed out in stacks of paper ready for wet signatures.

Be prepared. There is a lot of initialing and signing to do. It literally can take a couple of hours, and here are some of the documents you're going to have to sign off on:

- The title, which is the document declaring you the new owner
- Your mortgage papers
- Review of the contract
- Certifications relating to the property
- Closing-specific documents

You just have to bring two forms of ID to the closing table. The day prior to closing you will have to wire your funds in the total amount of the down payment, the closing costs, and any other expenses needed that have been outlined in advance for you. The closing attorney will send you secure wiring information by email, and it's good practice to call the closing attorney's office and verbally verify those very important instructions.

Because this long ceremony of a home closing is the bane of many people's existence, there are more and more options to do everything digitally and electronically from the comfort of your own home.

A common phishing scam is for a conman to send out fake wiring instructions to people they see bragging about buying a house on social media. Hackers can snoop your emails for keywords like "wire instructions" and "closing attorney" and send you incorrect wiring instructions. You don't want to get caught in this mess at the final C. I had this happen to a client and all I can say is neither one of us is planning to vacation in Nigeria anytime soon.

Whew, well, okay, let's assume you avoided that last pitfall and then you just start signing. You get the keys to your house at the end and you're the proud new owner of a House FIRE investment property and well on your way to be financially independent and retire early. Did it happen in less than three months? I bet it did.

After the actual closing, you're going to want to drive over to the property and check it out. This is a good time to introduce yourself to the tenant, if there is one. Let them know who you are and that their lease is still in effect and nothing is going to change except where they make payments to. Maybe you have already scheduled contractors or repairs to start ASAP on any work the house may need, but if not, get on that as time is money.

Congratulations, you've now done a complete circle around the Real Estate Investment Flywheel. Feels good doesn't it?

You can now begin on your next trip around as well, and in addition to taking a trip around the flywheel to find your next investment, you're actually starting another cycle as a new property owner—a flipper or a landlord. That's an entirely different cycle, and you're going to learn a lot on this journey, which I'll talk about in the next chapter.

But you have momentum now on property buying. Now that you've done it once, doesn't the thought of buying another property seem slightly easier the next time around? You are just working out the kinks at this stage. You potentially killed one or more bills with this purchase and that's huge. Let me know at @TheHouseOfAC about your first spin too. I want to celebrate with you.

A few more homes and you'll climb up the FIRE ranks and eventually get to HELLFIRE, if you want. That level still not for you? All good, I'm just glad you finally used one real estate purchase to put you on the path to FIRE. You are ahead of most who just dream about doing what you've done. But secretly, don't you want to be Lenny just a little bit?

15

"Alan, what does a FIRE-minded landlord do?"

As a new real estate investor, it's going to be hard to not buy a monocle, wear a black top hat, or grow a bushy white mustache. But you must resist. A lot of newbies trying to build their first real estate monopoly fall in this trap, and it just leads to endless arguments with your siblings.

So here you are. You finally made it to investor status either with a flip or a rental. So although this chapter seems to swing toward being a landlord, I'm actually going to focus on both scenarios.

Now I should point out that a single chapter not even dedicated to either of these topics on its own is hardly the definitive word on the subjects. Also, you chose me as your guide thus far and that's already showing some questionable decision-making skills. But I am up for the task. This synopsis is only meant to get you going on another trip around your Real Estate Investment Flywheel. So let's take a quick peek at some concepts that'll help you get started on that first property you just closed on.

You're a Landlord

In my view, owning rental property is the best of all worlds when it comes to wanting to FIRE (become financially independent and retire early). You're buying into something that immediately begins to pay you back. You get to capitalize on all five of the REI benefits: income, depreciation, principal paydown, appreciation, and leverage.

Although flips certainly can make you a lot of money quickly, they don't give you everything, but they're still awesome. I'm just saying that I like rentals the best as a long-term early retirement approach.

My first piece of advice is to learn how to be a landlord the traditional way, by actually being one. Manage your first few properties on your own if you can. You'll learn quickly what tenants are looking for in your market and what they don't want. You'll learn what certain plumbing repairs cost after meeting a few plumbers. You'll get an idea how long it takes to rent out an apartment. One of the most important aspects to running any kind of successful business is truly getting to know your customer.

In the case of being a landlord, your customer is the tenant. You know what they want in a property and that knowledge will help you with each new property you buy. You're learning the ropes, so to speak.

As an active landlord, you're also going to learn two important concepts: what a tenant needs from you and what you need from a tenant. Of course, we already know the obvious—they need a dry roof and you need a check.

Yet beyond that, you're going to want to understand what's expected on both sides and ways to keep the relations between you and your renters amiable and profitable.

You can tap into an ever-changing slew of options and software tools for mom-and-pop landlords like yourself. The software will post the vacancy ad online for you, take tenant applications online, run background checks, collect rent, and track repair items. Software developers have really made it easy for both tenants and landlords and make landlording not as time consuming as it used to be. Some software I have used to great success is Cozy.co, Zumper.com, AppFolio, and Buildium.

After trying out managing by yourself, if you want to hire a property management company, go for it. But at least then you'll know the landlording game a bit inside and out and you'll know how to keep tabs on your property management company.

Before I move onto renovations, here's a little tip that you can put to use if you think it'll help. We all know the power of the third party, right? In other words, sometimes people listen to a stranger who says the same thing you do. There are many reasons for this, but probably the biggest is that with the third party, there's no emotional investment. It makes life easier on all sides.

Well, the point I'm making is that you may want to approach your tenants not as the evil landlord, but rather as the agreeable property manager. In this way, the tenant and you aren't on diametrically opposite sides of the spectrum in some ways. It's not really even being dishonest. You are, in fact, the property manager. Yet in some cases, this relationship might make discussing repairs, late payments, moving dates, and whatever else less emotionally charged.

If you don't like something you can just say, "The owner asked me to tell you this." You then can both agree how unreasonable that idiotic owner is.

You're Flippin' Out

So you've just closed on that handyman special and you're standing in the driveway looking up and trying to figure out just how on earth you're going to turn this haunted house into a beautiful new home for somebody famous to be born in.

The first thing you're going to want to decide is if you're doing the work yourself, even in part, or if you are going to contract it out. There are two schools of thought here. First, doing it yourself obviously saves you money. If you've got the skills and the time, this might be a way for you to increase your profits and learn some skills along the way.

On the other hand, there's an old saying, or a question, rather: are you a handyman/woman or are you an investor? The truth is that most of us, unless we're full-time flippers, don't have the time to dedicate to a renovation. Doing a little in the evenings and on weekends is not only going to eat up a lot of your personal life, it's going to take considerably longer to flip the property. And with flips, one of the most important keys is speed.

I recommend hiring professionals to do the job. They have the skills and can dedicate full-time effort to your property. They can buy supplies in bulk across all their jobs, so they might not be as expensive as you think they will be. They're covered by insurance and can turn the work around far faster than a part-timer. And hopefully you've gotten a few quotes from reliable people prior to closing and can get on their schedule.

Get it all in writing: When you do hire contractors, make sure that everything is in writing. Don't leave anything to chance or to a handshake agreement made while standing in the driveway. You're going to want to set expectations right from the beginning.

Have a clear understanding of the work to be done as well as a time frame. Establish what happens if anything is late.

Establish how to handle cost increases, delays, and unexpected situations. Make sure everything is fair for both sides.

Budget for 25% cost increase and 50% time increase: Whatever you think your rehab costs are, add 25%. I know, that might sound like a lot, but believe me, having the money budgeted and not using it—or all of it—is far better than needing it and not having it. Like it or not, there are always unexpected costs and delays. Materials might cost more than you thought or weather might be a factor, or the contractors find something during the work that nobody expected with weight-bearing walls or shredded electrical or substandard plumbing.

And yeah, there will be delays. If you think the work is going to take sixty days, budget for ninety. A whole host of factors can slow a project down. Permitting, illness, the work being harder than you thought, and so on. Like the costs, if you assume a 50% longer time frame for completing the work, you'll be prepared for delays, and if you come in under schedule, then so much the better.

Carefully vet your contractors: I can't stress this one enough. Please don't just choose any old contractors. There are many good reasons to take your time and be thorough here.

First, you want to make sure that the work is going to be done correctly and as close to your budget and time as possible. Be wary of the large and well-known contractors. If somebody is heavily advertising their business, then that's going to be reflected in their rates. On the other hand, the cut-rate guy can be a problem too. Get at least three bids on your job. The guy who can start tomorrow is usually always a poor choice. There's a reason he can't find work.

The second reason to check out these contractors is that you're building a long-term relationship. If you find good ones, then you're going to use them over and over again. That's why getting multiple bids is a good idea. Additionally, take the time to talk with them. Get to know them and see if your personalities gel.

Make sure that you double-check everything. Not only should you get competing bids, you should also get references—and check them out. Get three references from each contractor. Yes, you're going to get their best three, but, still, it will give you an idea of what you can expect as well. Beware of any contractors who can't or don't provide references.

Make sure that whoever you choose has the right licenses and insurances in place. You know the term CYA right? Well, that's especially important here. You want to make sure that the contractors are licensed by the state, if applicable. You also want them to cover their own liabilities.

This is the ideal place to draw on your team. Remember that expert real estate agent you found a few chapters back? The one who's done a couple of flips themselves? Well, here is the opportunity to get references from that person to help you find quality and reliable contractors.

I've reached the end, or the beginning, in that you've made it all the way around your first Real Estate Investment Flywheel. So now what? Now we move on to your next property, which I'll explore in the next exciting chapter where we visit Lenny one last time as he is about to full-fledge House FIRE.

16

"Alan, I'm sitting pretty close to this FIRE!"

Ahhh, doesn't it feel good to have gone around the Real Estate Investing Flywheel for the first time and be able to enjoy life and make some s'mores? You've developed your strategy, chosen your product, and assembled your team. Because of all that, you're now the proud owner of your first deal.

Since this book is about getting to House FIRE and killing all your bills (being financially independent and retiring early), it's time to start thinking about your next deal.

Here's what's really cool about investing. With each successive deal, the whole process gets easier. It gets easier to qualify for another loan, easier to talk capital investors into working with you because you've now got hard proof to show them. You've done all of the ground work and now you've got the machinery in place. So that foundation makes it easier to find the next investment.

In order to make the journey around the REI Flywheel again that much faster and smoother, let's take a look at a few tips you can employ in order to accelerate your success.

Get your rental income on your tax returns: Aside from anything else, the income from your rental property adds to your overall gross income and will help you qualify for the next loan. Think about it. If you now own a house that rents for $1,500 per month, then you've just added $18,000 to your annual income. Yes, there are deductions, expenses, and notes to pay, but it still goes toward *qualification*.

 In a perfect world, you'd like your rental income to be at least 125% of the mortgage payment. Why is this? Well, it goes toward a term the bank likes to use called *debt service coverage ratio*—sometimes just shortened to debt service coverage or DSC.

DSC is usually calculated when you want to refinance. Basically, the bank wants to see that the income from a property is at least 1.25 times the debt. That gives them a comfortable cushion. If you're qualifying for another investment loan, the bank will look at this, so the greater the ratio, the less risky their next loan will be.

Also having your documented income on taxes makes you a bona fide real estate investor to a banker, one with experience, and they like lending money to experienced investors like yourself. So taking shortcuts and operating an all-cash off-the-books business is usually not going to benefit you in the long run, as it is also considered illegal and can get you in hot water.

Get preapproved again: Once you've got your new financials in place, go back to the bank and get preapproved for another loan. Figure out how much cash you have and what you qualify for so you can have laser beam focus on properties within your price range. You never want to go out into the cold without having a sound understanding of your financial situation and what you need to improve it. You have a twelve-month clock ticking to secure your second home, so now is not the time to dillydally.

Recycle your profits: What if you bought a flip? You don't have rental income to show, so what then? Well, you will have profits from your first deal and you will have to pay capital gains tax, so they'll be on your tax returns no matter what.

I suggest that if you've done your first flip that you put all of the remaining cash back into the next one. When it comes to flipping, cash is king.

This might seem like it flies in the face of the whole leverage concept. In truth, though, when it comes to fix and flips, leverage is great, but cash is greater. Because the deal is turned around in three to four months, the idea is quick in and quick out. So the more of your own capital you can bring to bear on a deal, the more benefits you'll enjoy.

Imagine if you find a property that needs $40K worth of work and is selling for $80K. You calculate an ARV of $150K and your high comps suggest that it could sell for between $160K and $165K if the market remains hot. With all expenses and such, you figure it'll cost you $130K to buy, fix, and hold the property until you sell it.

Now, would you rather borrow $100K and wait for loan approval and so on? What if you had the $130K in the bank already? How much faster could you snap up that deal? How much of a better price could you offer the seller with a seven- to fourteen-day close all-cash deal?

Yes, Alan, you say, but before you said that I should go and buy two or three deals with my cash, rather than one. Yes, and I meant it, for rentals. And when you're a little more experienced, then you can do this for flips too. However, for now, I'd recommend doing only one flip at a time. So in this case, the more you build your cash pile, the more effective you'll be. After about four or five flips, with a strong team and a solid grasp on material and labor costs, then you can leverage and do four to five at the same time.

Catch and repeat: Now it's time to find another catch. You already know what to do and what you're looking for. I think you'll find that the second time around the flywheel is going to be so much more comfortable for you. Just follow the steps I've already outlined. Repeat the process exactly as I've talked about for another successful investment.

I think now you're ready for some of the next-level stuff. The tricks and tips that the big wheels know and that accelerates their investing businesses into the stratosphere. In the final section coming up, I'm going to give you a sneak peek at what's next and what lies in your future. It's exciting stuff and I think you'll be amazed at what you can achieve.

The Portfolio

After you buy your second property, you will have unlocked the portfolio achievement. You'll hear the phrase "real estate portfolio" a lot more often now. That basically means you have more than one property, which could be land, single family homes, multifamily homes, or any combination of real estate holdings that are not your primary residence. But why does having a real estate portfolio matter?

With a portfolio you have more options than if you just had one property. You can package them together and do cool things if you want. Let's have a look at Lenny's portfolio and I'll show you.

- 123 Main Street. $275,000, duplex. Gets $1,850 in rent total. No mortgage on it.
- 130 Main Street. $300,000 duplex. Gets $2,000 in rent total. $275,000 mortgage on it.

- 789 Rural Road. $100,000, single family house. Gets $600 in rent. $60,000 mortgage on it.
- 666 Hellfire Goal Boulevard. $350,000, triplex. Gets $4,000 in total rent. $150,000 mortgage on it.
- 99 Tower Lane. $200,000 studio apartment. Gets $750 in rent. $150,000 mortgage on it.

So Lenny didn't really have one specific category he invested in it seems. He has apartments, single families, and multifamily. Some of the addresses are in the center of the city and some are out in the sticks. Portfolios work much better if they are in the same location and of the same product type, but let's see how it is performing for ol' scatterbrained Lenny and what his options are.

Lenny puts his numbers into a spreadsheet to give them a closer look. He rounds his numbers for now and just ignores the tax breaks he receives and the principal paydown he gets on his four mortgages across his five properties.

	Type	Value	Mortgage	Interest Rate	Rent	Cash Flow
123 Main	Duplex	$275,000	$0	0%	$1,850	$1,500
130 Main	Duplex	$300,000	$275,000	7%	$2,000	$25
789 Rural	Single family	$100,000	$ 60,000	4%	$600	$150
666 Hellfire	Triplex	$350,000	$150,000	8%	$4,000	$2,000
99 Tower	Studio apt	$200,000	$150,000	3.5%	$750	$0
Totals		$1,225,000	$635,000		$9,200	$3,675

Lenny is doing well with his modest five-rental portfolio in five years. With $3,675 of monthly cash flow, he can live off $44,100 of expenses a year. That's major House FIRE territory and a huge achievement. Way to go, Lenny!

Let's assume Lenny has everything on thirty-year mortgages and they are in various stages of being paid off. Lenny has House FIRE'd, and if he does nothing but wait until the tenants pay off the balances on his four open mortgages, then he will eventually have $9,200 of rent coming in, or $110,400 a year. He'll probably have $30,000 a year in maintenance, property taxes, and repairs. That leaves him around $80,000 a year, and he has almost reached Fat FIRE level. And remember, we aren't even looking at any savings, 401(k)s, or retirement funds Lenny may have to his name. He will most likely Fat FIRE on rental income alone in a few years with no worry about a FIRE number.

If we assume he put 20 to 25% down payment on each property, he Fat FIRE'd with $275,000. Much better than saving $2.5 million (25 x $100,000 in annual expenses) to hit a daunting FIRE number in order to retire. Sure the $275,000 took some time to work its magic, but it most likely would have taken a much longer time for Lenny to save $2.5 million.

So let's go back to his portfolio. There is a multifamily investor named Alisha calling around town, and she only buys multifamilies within three blocks of the downtown subway station. Her very strict criteria make it easy for her to evaluate a deal, and every time Lenny talks to other investors, they tell him, "Oh, Alisha is looking for what you got if you ever want to sell."

"Yeah, yeah, I know Alisha," Lenny says. "She's already called me. We use the same contractor. Not sure if I want to sell yet. I just retired."

But does being retired make it a bad time for Lenny to sell? He's happy with his cash flow, there is no way he has more than $3,675 in expenses a month, his primary residence was paid off long ago. And his wealth will go up just by waiting via principal paydown. These properties will definitely hold their value or appreciate some more based on location alone. Lenny talks to Alisha just to feel her out on her price.

Alisha knows the value of her product inside and out, but there isn't much inventory for her to buy, so she's willing to pay a slight premium to get what she wants. She has $250,000 between her and her investors to invest after flipping a few homes, and she wants to transition to long-term rentals now. Also Alisha's connections with a local commercial lender give her preferential deals only on purchases of five units or more. Alisha needs to bundle Lenny's properties together to make seven units (duplex, duplex, and a triplex) instead of buying them individually to hit that threshold.

Alisha offers $950,000 for his portfolio of three multifamilies, $25,000 more than they would sell individually on the open market. She's not interested in the other two rentals as they don't fit her investing criteria. If only Lenny had focused his efforts in one specific combination he could have leveraged his portfolio a little more.

Lenny says he needs time to think about the offer. If he sells to Alisha, Lenny would take home about $525,000 after paying off the mortgages. Lenny never thought he'd see a $500,000 check before. Actually, after taxes, it will be more like a $425,000 check.

With $425,000 he could pay off the mortgages on his studio apartment and single family rentals. That would leave him with $210,000 and bring his incoming cash flow to around $1,350 a month. It's still a solid income and maybe he plays it safe in retirement and keeps that extra cash in his bank account. Or maybe he takes that $210,000 and buys another house in the outskirts for cash and rents it out for $650 to bring up his income to $2,000. Buying properties with no mortgage? Lenny has forgotten about the whole balcony incident it seems.

Lenny looks the numbers over and over, and even though he's selling his portfolio for more than $25,000 than they are worth, he can't paint a picture where he benefits in this situation. If he sells, his cash flow goes down and his wait to Fat FIRE strategy goes out the window. (Good recovery, Lenny.)

Then Lenny remembers reading the book by that genius author Alan Corey and in it was something about upgrading his portfolio into bigger properties via a 1031 like-kind exchange. It was in the last chapter, he recalls.

Lenny rereads that amazing book and then researches 1031s on his own because he's diligent and it never hurts to fact check those crazy real estate gurus. Lenny finds that if he takes all the money he makes on the sale of an investment property and reinvests it into another property, then he can avoid a tax hit.

That $100,000 that went poof directly to the government in his earlier calculations is no more. If he buys another property, or another portfolio of properties, from his proceeds of selling to Alisha and he puts it back into real estate, then he can defer the tax gains.

Lenny could take that $525,000 and buy a few more properties with it and that gets him looking. He has learned over his real estate investing career that having as many units as possible under one roof gets him the most bang for his buck. He can condense his efforts to one building instead of being spread out over a large geographic area. He would only have one roof to replace, one yard to maintain, one water and sewer main pipe to have to replace one day. Plus a vacancy wouldn't hurt as much. Shit, he really did read Alan's book.

Lenny knows there will be about $25,000 in closing costs on a new purchase, so he's already rounding his purchase power to *only* $500,000. Eye roll.

So with $500,000 to spend, that's a 25% down payment on a $2 million property. There are a lot of options for that.

In Lenny's town, two mill would buy him a twenty-unit apartment building full of two-bedroom/one-bath units. Lenny calls a commercial agent who has one off-market complex for that price and it generates $25,000 in rent roll. So Lenny runs new numbers.

First, Lenny takes a moment to reflect that his entire portfolio at the moment is valued at $1,225,000 and just by selling three properties as a portfolio he could buy a property that is worth almost double that by using more leverage this time around. There has to be a catch and this seems too easy, so he's being extra studious on the calculations.

A commercial loan for a massive $1.5 million mortgage at 7% with a seven-year balloon payment would cost Lenny about $10,000 a month. Seems unachievable at first glance and too much risk to Lenny going into retirement. Lenny's income would not allow him to qualify to purchase this property alone, but this is a commercial deal, and commercial lenders primarily look at the numbers of the building in evaluating a deal. So let's peek at Lenny's spreadsheet and see if trading up makes any financial sense for him.

	3 property multifamily portfolio	20-unit apartment complex
Value	$950,000 to Angela	$2,000,000 off-market
Mortgage Balance	$425,000	$1,500,000
Equity	$525,000	$500,000
Monthly Rental Income	$7,850	$25,000
Monthly Mortgage Payment	$3,000	$10,000
Property Management	$0, self-manages	$2,500
Monthly Property Taxes	$1,250	$3,500
Monthly Insurance	$200	$2,000
Monthly Repair Budget	$500	$2,250
Monthly Vacancy Budget	$650	$2,500
Cash Flow	**$2,250**	**$2,250**

So what do you think? Does Lenny trade? It matches cash flow for cash flow so is there a clear winner?

Does it make sense for Lenny to take on more debt as he enters early retirement? The new purchase would not only 3.5x his current debt obligations but it would reset Lenny's mortgage to another thirty years of payback. Lenny is sixty-five now and may not make it to ninety-five since he wants to live on the edge in early retirement and take up microdosing

LSD while skydiving over active volcanoes. (Pickle-ball is over. This is the new thing all the retirees are doing.)

If he doesn't sell his small portfolio, Lenny can pay off his other properties' mortgages in about ten years by plugging his cash flow back into paying down the mortgages quickly using the Dave Ramsey–approved way. You know, the dumb thing every retiree does against their better interest. But it just sort of feels safe to Lenny to enter retirement with no debt at all and live free as a bird, just not the most financially savvy bird.

Sorry, bear with me. I really want to drive this no-mortgage point home before we say goodbye. Most people will assume that billionaires are experts with money, right? Their net worth is basically a scorecard of their financial acumen. Do we agree on that?

Now, how many billionaires do you think have real estate investments paid off in cash? I'll tell you, it's zero. I know this because being a real estate agent I've seen the contracts, I've seen the closing docs, and I've been involved in a myriad of deals with ultra-high-net-worth buyers as a real estate agent. And I'll let out their secret: they all get loans.

Sure, having all their money in a bank means that their interest rate is about 2% less than what regular folks get, but they also do have the means to pay all cash for these properties and every single time choose not to. Billys (my new nickname for billionaires) know that paying in cash or even trying to pay them off in cash later is a poor financial move. So if you don't trust me, trust your favorite Billy that it's the right decision to have a mortgage.

Speaking of Billys, which Lenny is not. If Len-Len does sell all his multifamilies, he doesn't have to self-manage those seven units anymore as he can afford a property manager and then has more free time to dedicate to drug-influenced skydiving and to those neglected bald eagle eggs in his attic.

He can't make up his mind. Does it take traditional FIRE advice or my newly improved House FIRE advice?

Lenny reviews the numbers again and notices the new purchase has tenants paying down his $1.5 million mortgage for him instead of tenants paying down a $425,000 mortgage. That's a huge difference. And if this new giant loan balance ever gets paid off, he'll have rental income of at least $25,000 a month.

Chances are, though, he'll get those rents up and expenses down over time and be primed for HELLFIRE. Sure he'll be ninety-five, but he'll be the biggest baller in his retirement home, which has always been his dream. He still has two other properties with a total of $90,000 in equity he could 1031 also to really make the grannies ooh and ahh over his FIRE balls.

But thinking short term and being a little more pragmatic, Lenny really thinks both the rents and property values will appreciate about 10% over the next three to five years with all the growth his city is seeing. If this comes to fruition, then he gains about $85,772 in equity by keeping his three-property portfolio and his cash flow would go up $200 a month. That's hard to give up. Or is it?

When Lenny compares that same 10% increase in rents and property value scenario with his new twenty-unit purchase, he sees his equity would go up $185,000 and his cash flow would increase $2,000 a month, it becomes an easy decision. Lenny does the right thing and sells to Alisha (after writing a thank-you letter to Alan Corey for his wisdom).

And there you have it. Lenny got rich dreaming instead of dreaming about getting rich with just a few houses on his path to House FIRE. Now it's your turn. You have the entire playbook right here in your hands. Go out and execute. Become a Billy. And remember your ol' pal Alan when you have more money than you can count. He'll be buying volcanoes for you to skydive over.

What Those Words Mean

Appreciation: The value a property has risen either through your improvement of the property, the overall economy, or local exterior changes that made the property more desirable. Example: My spouse appreciated the effort I put forth in renovating the stinky basement into a testosterone-filled man cave since the house appreciated in value because of it.

ARM: Adjustable rate mortgage. If you don't have a fixed-rate mortgage, your interest rate will adjust (up or down) after a certain number of years. Example: I have a five-year ARM on my investment property because I didn't fully understand Alan's book about why this can be a risky way to invest.

ARV: After-rehab value. What you think the house will be worth when you are done with renovations. Example: After Lenny went to rehab, his self-worth increased, just like a house does with some self-love.

Balloon: A balloon payment is the date when the mortgage note is due. You might have a thirty-year fixed amortization note with a five-year balloon, which means you are charged each month as if you have a thirty-year note, but in five years you have to pay the remaining balance in full or refinance to a new loan. Example: My career as a balloon-artist was not stable, so when my balloon payment came due on my mortgage, I had no option but to skip town and join the circus. I'm now working on a book called *Clown FIRE* about how to fit thirteen people into a car in order to maximize your return as an UberPool driver.

Barista FIRE: Typically defined as you are able to FIRE with a part-time job or if in a couple, one partner works full-time while the other partner is able to FIRE. Example: I get free health insurance by working part-time at the national coffee chain. If I lived in another country that actually provided free national healthcare, I'd be fully FIRE'd.

Billys: Billionaires, the real estate investors who can pay cash for properties but don't. Example: I know Alan Corey would share his tremendous wealth for good and not evil so I'm going to support him until he becomes a Billy.

BRRRR: What you say when it's cold outside. Or Buy, Rehab, Rent, Refinance, and Repeat, a strategy by uber-popular real estate investor and *BiggerPockets* podcaster Brandon Turner. Example: I BRRRR'd this worn-down property with no heat I bought in Alaska by adding a furnace, steam shower, sauna, fireplace, and a solarium to make sure the appraisal came in sky high when I went to refinance.

Cap Rate: Capitalization rate formula to evaluate a property to quickly see the rate of return that will be generated on an investment. Cap Rate = Net Operating Income/Purchase Price of Property. Example: I almost get capped every time I drive by my investment house, but the cap rate is 20% so it's worth it.

Cash-on-Cash Return: Calculates the return on the actual money you put in yourself. NOI minus mortgage payments/down payment. Example: I put $0 in this property so my cash-on-cash return is infinite like a financial superhero that should be cast in the next *Avengers: Infinity War* movie.

Coast FIRE: The point in FIRE where you have hit your FIRE number but choose to keep working (coasting) and no longer have to add to savings. Example: I'm a rich bitch, so I'm not going to work late or on weekends anymore, boss. But I do still want to keep working here, so don't get too offended.

Debt Service Coverage Ratio or DSC: Measurement of how much monthly cash flow covers the amount of monthly debt payments on a property. Example: LOL, ICYMI my DSC is 1.5, YMMV. HTH.

Equity: Your property value minus what you owe on it. Example: I earned my equity in the property via sweat equity of my hard work to renovate it unlike Lenny's sweatpants equity where he just sat back and put in money but didn't lift a finger.

Fat FIRE: $100,000 in expenses or a FIRE number of $2.5 million. Example: Being fat and happy is what my tycoon corporate mentor taught me before his cardiac arrest.

FIRE: Financial independence, retire early. The topic of this book, in case you didn't know. Start reading from the front of the book next time. Check out my free basic FIRE course at www.TheHouseOfAC.com if you want to be financially independent and retire early.

FIRE Number: Typically calculated as your annual expenses x 25. If you have this amount in savings, you have reached FIRE and can live off a 4% withdrawal rate per year moving forward. Example: I hit my FIRE Number because I wanted to go the slow route to financial independence instead of the simpler and faster way of House FIRE.

HELLFIRE: Having Every Luxury in Life FIRE. Having $500,000 annual expenses or $41,666 a month in expenses covered by passive income. Example: They call it HELLFIRE because in this hell you are still 2,000 years away from being a Billy.

HELOC: Home equity line of credit is a way to withdraw money from the equity of your property. Example: Using a HELOC as a down payment on another property is what a real estate investor would do. Using a HELOC to lease a Lamborghini is what a social media influencer would do.

HOA: Homeowners association. Example: I like to surround myself with power-hungry volunteers who like to impede my progress in real estate, so I only invest in neighborhoods with HOA restrictions.

House FIRE: A way to FIRE (be financially independent and retire early) using mortgages to leverage your wealth. Cash flow of a property is used to cover your bills and allows you to FIRE with about one-fifth the money of other forms of FIRE. It also is the only FIRE method where your living expenses can increase in retirement as your cash flow increases simultaneously as your debt obligations decrease over time. Example: Because he House FIRE'd at forty, I now have to deal with Alan Corey's midlife crisis via his ubiquitous books, courses, and podcasts.

Lean FIRE: Typically defined as having $25,000 a year in living expenses and a FIRE number of $625,000.

Example: While on shrooms, I gained empathy and denounced capitalism so my boomer parents don't really understand my Lean FIRE life.

LLC: Limited liability company. Example: I created an LLC to protect me from getting sued for providing too much Viagra to my jacuzzi-hopping tenants once they got erections lasting more than four hours.

LTV: Loan to value. Typically a bank will lend 75 to 80% loan to value on a property. Example: My bank said they'd give me 75% LTV on my ARV of my BRRRR, which means I've now cracked the code of investor speak.

MLS: Multiple Listing Service is the database where real estate agents list properties for sale that eventually populates to all the other real estate websites. Example: I know you saw a house on Zillow that is for sale but the MLS says it sold two weeks ago, so unfortunately you don't have the most accurate information.

NOI: Net operating income. Gross or total income minus expenses. Example: I make $100,000 in gross rental income, but what I capture after filtering it through an expensive net is what I really make in profit.

PITI: Principal, interest, tax, and insurance. A mortgage payment often includes all four areas. Example: It's a pity when my tenant's rental income does not cover my PITI payments in full.

PMI: Private mortgage insurance, or an extra fee the bank charges when you put a low down payment on a property. Example: I have to pay a little extra for PMI to borrow more money, but no big deal if the numbers still make sense as an investment.

REI: Real estate investing. Example: I avoid Taco Tuesday nights at Dia's REI events because it's just bad food with loan sharks attending.

REI Flywheel: Real Estate Investing Flywheel. A four-part way to visualize your investing efforts and something to which you can refer and keep track of your progress. Consists of knowledge, confidence, action, and experience. Created by Alan Corey who can't let a moment go by without giving himself credit for things. Example: The REI Flywheel is so simple, I ended up House FIRE'ing after five rentals.

ROI: Return on investment. The whole point of this book. Example: The reward of my efforts into House FIRE returned the ROI I knew I could achieve.

Acknowledgments

Like all things grand, it took a superstar team for me to pull this book off. It took the editorial input of Scott Cook, Eric Hughes, Danielle Anderson, and Sandra Wendel to help shape my ramblings into something people would want to read.

Damien Scott and John Grosso are the greatest real estate partners one can have. I get the pleasure of learning from you every day.

Weslee Knapp, I appreciate you being a great mentor and encouraging me on every twist and turn I take on my real estate journey.

Kudos to my family for the freedom to write during a worldwide pandemic. Sadia, you make it easy for me to be successful. Zain, Nyle, and Ellis, you make it worth the effort.

Lastly, thank you, reader. It's the last page of the book and you are obviously still craving for more, so go to www.TheHouseOfAC.com and continue your real estate education there. Also all my dad jokes are reduced by at least 50% online.

Meet Alan Corey

Alan Corey is an Atlanta-based entrepreneur, speaker, writer, real estate agent, investor, and consultant. Alan's previous books *A Million Bucks by 30* and *The Subversive Job Search* teach financial basics and out-of-the-box job hunting techniques.

When Alan isn't talking about real estate and money, he's trying to start conversations about these subjects with his wife and three children. (The pets get a lot of unsolicited advice as well.)

To find out more about Alan, visit www.TheHouseOfAC.com or follow him on all social media channels at @TheHouseOfAC.